The
Power *of*
One Thought

Celebrating
30 Years of Publishing
in India

The
Power *of*
One Thought

Master Your Mind, Master Your Life

BK Shivani

HarperCollins *Publishers* India

First published in India by HarperCollins *Publishers* 2023
4th Floor, Tower A, Building No. 10, DLF Cyber City,
DLF Phase II, Gurugram, Haryana – 122002
www.harpercollins.co.in

2 4 6 8 10 9 7 5 3 1

P-ISBN: 978-93-5699-333-4
E-ISBN: 978-93-5699-332-7

Typeset in 11/14.5 Minion Pro at
Manipal Technologies Limited, Manipal

Printed and bound at
Thomson Press (India) Ltd

Contents

Preface

OM SHANTI. GREETINGS OF PEACE.

Visualize waking up tomorrow morning and going about the entire day, absolutely happy with everything—with yourself, your family, your home, your career, your social circle, your city ... your world. You find several imperfections in them, but you remain calm and contented.

How different will your tomorrow be from today?

Everything you do in life has an underpinned pursuit of feeling peace, love and happiness. But today despite working hard, these emotions seem elusive—now you feel nice, the next moment you do not. Most of us ride an emotional roller-coaster from time to time. But we refuse to take responsibility for our emotions. We find it easier to blame the world for how we feel, and hence say, 'Life is a roller-coaster'.

Your world is not somewhere out there. It starts from within your mind. Your mind creates thoughts which in turn create your feelings and emotions. This book nudges and reconnects you to the source of emotions—your thoughts. Embark on this inner journey to learn the intricate workings and powers of your mind. Learn to channelize it so that you can shift from impulsive reactions, to choosing the right response in every scene of life. Unlock your potential to think right and remain calm, no matter what situation you are in.

How long will you need to empower and transform yourself? Choosing the right response is a gradual process requiring attention and awareness. One day you may accept people easily, forgive their mistakes and let go. The next day you might unintentionally slip back into the earlier reaction of retaliating angrily. Ensure that you do not create guilt or criticize yourself. Even if people around you start judging you for faltering, do not suspect your progress. You alone will know how far you have come, so appreciate your journey for the small and big changes you brought about. Transformation may happen in small steps but that is a huge achievement.

By creating a change in how you respond, you contribute to changing the world. Each time you shift from ego to humility, stress to calm, anger to compassion, hurt to forgiveness, worry to care, expectations to acceptance, holding on to letting go, guilt to realization, comparison to self-respect, competition to cooperation, attachment to love, not only you change … your world changes.

When you change, the world changes. Be the change to begin the change.

BK Shivani
15 May 2023

1

Ready to Set Yourself Free?

LET US BEGIN WITH A SHORT STORY—THE TALE OF A little eaglet which was perched on a tree branch, its curling talons firmly gripping the wood. A boy passing by saw it desperately flapping its wings to fly but failing. There was more than enough momentum for the bird to move through the air and fly but it just did not take off. After a few minutes, it finally gave up. The boy went closer and asked the exhausted eaglet what had happened. The bird mumbled, 'I tried so hard to fly but this branch is holding me back. It is not letting me go.' The startled boy pointed out, 'What are you saying? The branch is not holding you. It is you who has clutched onto it. Just let go of the branch and you will easily fly.'

Many of us are familiar with this story. Oftentimes, our own life experiences resonate with it. Within us we have all the emotions we wish to feel—peace, happiness, kindness

1

and contentment. So we are free to experience them at every moment. But somehow we seem to be oblivious of this freedom. We chase after these emotions and often feel that something holds us back from accessing them. And much like the eaglet, we remain emotionally stuck and become disheartened.

If peace, happiness, kindness and contentment are our inherent qualities, today, let us take a moment to ask ourselves:

- *I can be calm in a crisis. WHY do I panic and get stressed?*
- *I can be happy even when I don't get what I want. WHY do I feel so upset?*
- *I can be kind when someone makes a mistake. WHY do I get so angry?*
- *I can be contented with my life. WHY do I feel so dissatisfied?*

WHY are we unable to regulate our emotions when it matters the most? What is this emotional bondage we are not letting go of, depriving ourselves of the very happiness we seek? Let us first recognize the emotional bondage. Thereafter we shall work on setting ourselves free.

Recall the time when you last felt angry at someone. You had believed your anger was completely justified and natural, as the other person was clearly wrong. Now, reflect closely: Could you have responded another way?

Replay the entire scene on the screen of your mind. It is the same situation and the other person commits the same mistake. Bring the focus on you now, and visualize yourself choosing a right response, an emotionally healthy response.

What would it be? What will your thoughts be? How will you speak? How will your tone be? What will your body language be?

You might have visualized yourself being peaceful and stable. You do not lose self-control this time. You remain assertive, not angry. Your words are reformative, not accusatory. Your stability empowers the other person to realize his mistake and change.

But when the incident had occurred in the past, why had you reacted impulsively? What was holding you back from adopting peace then? It was your emotional dependency. It was your belief that your response depended on the situation and on people's behaviour, and not on you. You had believed you did not have the choice to respond any other way. When you had justified anger, perhaps other people present on the scene had endorsed your reactive behaviour as natural and normal.

It has been deeply embedded in our minds that our emotions and behaviour depend on situations and other people. This dependency is akin to the eaglet believing that the branch was holding it and hence it did not have the choice of flying away. But when you reflect on the scene now, in retrospect, you can see that you are not emotionally dependent and that you have the choice of responding differently. This wisdom is akin to the eaglet realizing that the branch was not holding it back and it could fly.

No matter how deeply we believe that we are dependent on external factors, the truth is that we have complete freedom to choose our response. This is called Emotional Independence.

Emotional Dependency: Is It Bad for You?

Some of us might wonder if it will make any difference whether we are dependent or independent. After all, we have lived with dependency for years. But it does make a vast difference.

Unfortunately, the seeds of emotional dependence were sown quite early on in our lives. Recall the school essays you wrote about the happiest day of your life. You might have written about a birthday party, a vacation or an award you received. This means that right from childhood, we permitted ourselves to feel happy only when a pleasant event occurred. And we were led to believe it was natural to feel unhappy or upset when things were not favourable.

Scenes come and go, whether it is something that happened today or a memory from a year ago. In retrospect, we often regret:

- *I should not have reacted that way. I should have handled it differently.*
- *I could have kept quiet and let go of what happened.*
- *Why did I worry so much? Everything turned out fine in the end.*

As we move forward, we realize there was another way to respond to the given person or situation. We did not choose a response but were only reacting based on the situation or the people involved.

There are two worlds we live in: an outer world and an inner world.

- The outer world comprises situations, people and their behaviour, relationships, work, material possessions, natural resources and even our body (or physical health).
- The inner world comprises thoughts, feelings, intentions and memories.

Today, we want situations to be perfect for us to be happy, calm and stable. So we are waiting for the outside world to become perfect so that our inner world can be perfect too.

Think about this: back in the day, we were able to live reasonably happily even with dependencies, as the outer world was more or less predictable. There was an element of certainty in health, in relationships, in the economy, in the average life span and so on. We did experience tension once in a while but overcame it easily. In the last two decades, we have witnessed enormous uncertainty in the outer world. The changes have been rapid and drastic. This means situations outside are uncertain. By making our state of mind dependent on them, our reactions have also become uncertain. Since both outer and inner worlds have become uncertain, we are often left feeling powerless, helpless, anxious, insecure and fearful. This is why stress has become the norm, depression and anxiety are common, diabetes is rampant, cancer is on the rise, divorce seems an easier option … it is a long list.

Given these circumstances, we have two options:

Option 1: We create an outer world which functions completely the way we want and then we let the inner world be dependent on it. When the outer world becomes perfect, we will experience lasting happiness and health.

Option 2: We realize that our inner world is independent of the outer world. We start creating certainty (and stability) in our responses to the uncertainties of the outer world. With this option, we will naturally remain happy and healthy.

Option 1 seems impossible since the outer world of people and situations does not always function the way we want. But Option 2 is completely achievable. Therefore the time has come for us to bring the inner world under our control so that no matter what situation comes up suddenly from the outer world—it could be that someone betrays us or behaves badly, our business crashes, our body develops an illness or we lose a family member—we still have the ability to remain emotionally stable and respond in the right way.

The word 'responsibility' can be broken down into 'response' and 'ability', signifying our capability to respond to every scene. If we create a list of our responsibilities, it would include aspects like family, home, career, finances, achievements and so on. Today, let us add our own names right on top of that list, since our emotional state is our first responsibility in every scene of life.

Emotional Independence: What's It All About?

The word 'independence' says it all. Consider 'in' and 'dependence'. 'In' means 'inside'. What is 'inside'? I, the being, the energy—we can call it light, consciousness, power, spirit or soul. I am dependent only on the one 'in'-side, which means on the self (myself) ... I am dependent only on myself. But if I keep pointing at someone else, then I am not in-dependent. Instead, I am out-dependent. In-dependence means to be dependent only on the one inside.

Scenes are only a stimulus, and we always have the choice of response. Till we experience the emotional independence of choosing our right response consciously, we will not be able to experience the happiness, peace, calmness and contentment that we are all looking for.

Ask yourself: what am I ready to do to gift myself emotional independence?

For now, take note of the words 'emotional dependence' and be prepared to get rid of them soon. This book is a journey to liberate you from all forms of emotional dependencies. As you progress through the chapters and internalize the content, you will move closer to the freedom that you deserve.

It All Begins with Your Thoughts

Every scene in our life demands a response. Our very first response is always a thought, followed by a feeling. Some responses are only internal, such as thoughts and feelings.

At other times, our thoughts are translated into words and behaviours as well. But it all happens so fast that we are not even aware that we first created a thought, which then manifested as our words and behaviours.

The origin of our behavioural responses lies in the most basic of our internal responses: our thoughts. Our thoughts create our feelings, words and behaviour, in that order. If we take care of our thoughts, we will not need to be careful with our words and behaviours. **Right thoughts will always create the right response.** Sometimes we create thoughts of irritation, impatience, hurt or jealousy but we manage to speak sweetly. Let us master the art of creating the right thoughts in response to every scene. We will then not find the need to suppress our thoughts or hide our feelings. This brings transparency, authenticity and integrity. Don't we all appreciate it when people are authentic, speaking what they think and doing what they say?

Get Off the Emotional Roller Coaster

Let us do a simple activity. Run through these sample scenarios and responses in your mind. Check if this is how you respond when things go right and even when they do not.

❏ You wake up in the morning feeling fresh and relaxed. You get ready to leave but your breakfast is delayed by fifteen minutes and it is not to your taste. You eat hurriedly, while angrily giving the cook an earful. You leave for office in a bad mood.

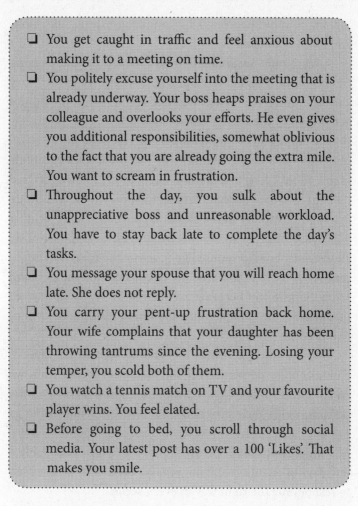

❏ You get caught in traffic and feel anxious about making it to a meeting on time.

❏ You politely excuse yourself into the meeting that is already underway. Your boss heaps praises on your colleague and overlooks your efforts. He even gives you additional responsibilities, somewhat oblivious to the fact that you are already going the extra mile. You want to scream in frustration.

❏ Throughout the day, you sulk about the unappreciative boss and unreasonable workload. You have to stay back late to complete the day's tasks.

❏ You message your spouse that you will reach home late. She does not reply.

❏ You carry your pent-up frustration back home. Your wife complains that your daughter has been throwing tantrums since the evening. Losing your temper, you scold both of them.

❏ You watch a tennis match on TV and your favourite player wins. You feel elated.

❏ Before going to bed, you scroll through social media. Your latest post has over a 100 'Likes'. That makes you smile.

Reflect on the responses above: being furious at the cook, critical of the traffic, resentful of the boss, disgruntled at work, irritated about the spouse's silence, annoyed with the child, happy for the player who won and pleased about the validation on social media. Can you see a clear pattern of looking at other people's behaviour or at external situations and reacting to them?

A reaction is 'automated' where we act without pausing to choose how to be. A response is where we consciously choose how to be. When we choose a response, we do not get swayed by the quality of the situation.

The ripple effect of our impulsive reactions in the chain of daily events is also noteworthy. The mood created in one scene, if not corrected, is more likely to get carried forward into the next. Suppose we face a situation with anger. There is a high possibility that a slight trigger in the next incident will again push us to react angrily. Unless we consciously choose a different response like peace or calmness, our angry reaction is likely to spill into the next scene, and the next and so on. Soon, anger becomes an 'automated' reaction as we go through the day complaining about and blaming the things that don't go our way.

Usually, when it comes to making 'big-impact' choices like selecting a degree, career, life partner or investments, we take the time to respond. We first introspect, identify all the options, weigh their pros and cons, and then choose. But in everyday life, we mostly react to scenes in impulsive ways. Making a conscious effort to choose a response takes only a few days of attention and awareness. Thereafter, we get used to responding the right way in every scene.

If we ask ourselves what we desire the most in life, the most common answers would be: love, happiness, peace and power. What we want to experience is what we need to create in response to every scene. For only when we create it, can we experience it and radiate it into the world. This is our power and potential. But if we keep blaming circumstances, saying, 'He avoided me though he knew I was there. How could he do that?', 'She was rude to me …', 'No one cares for me …' or 'Why is the weather so bad today?', then with each thought, we are drifting away from the very happiness and peace we seek.

What Do Dependencies Look Like?

When someone asks us why we are upset or dull, we readily point fingers outwards:

- *With such a chaotic situation it is natural to feel distressed.*
- *Their words were upsetting.*
- *The weather is so depressive.*

Even when anyone asks us why we are happy or peaceful, we credit external factors:

- *The occasion was such that I obviously felt happy.*
- *I got his phone call and instantly felt good.*
- *Since she is polite, I enjoy her company.*

When someone speaks lovingly, we feel happy. If they change their tone, we feel hurt. So who is controlling our feelings? Who holds the remote control to our mind? We believe it to be in the hands of other people. This does not just include the people we know. It could even be a stranger on the road. Recall how furious we get when someone overtakes our vehicle from the wrong side or honks at a traffic signal. But we blame that person for our anger. This means we do not even take responsibility for our reactions.

We no longer realize that we are not choosing how to respond—we feel like we reacted automatically. In other words, we take the remote control of our mind and hand it over even to random individuals. In fact, everyone other than us seems to hold our remote control today. It is now time to wake up to reality and remind the self: **I am the master of my mind. I am the creator of my every thought and feeling.**

Let us examine the extent of our dependency. Tick the option closest to your own thoughts, conversations or behaviour. You may mark multiple options for each question. Take your time, since each line of this exercise involves reflection.

- What makes you angry, upset, hurt, happy or loving?
  - ❏ It depends on who it is.
  - ❏ It depends on what they did.
  - ❏ It depends on how important they are to me.
  - ❏ It depends on what happened.

- Is there any person, place or object about which you say, 'I cannot do without'?
  - ❏ I cannot live without him/her. I want to be with him/her all the time.

- ❏ I can't do without my annual vacation. It's a must.
- ❏ My heart skips a beat if I don't find my phone in my bag.
- ❏ I don't even get sleep if I miss watching this TV show every night.

- Is there any habit or addiction about which you say, 'It's not in my control'?
  - ❏ Sweets are my weakness. I can't resist the temptation.
  - ❏ Smoking has become a habit. It's no longer in my control.
  - ❏ My mornings begin with this news channel.
  - ❏ My day does not go well if it does not begin with coffee.

- When the outcome of a situation does not go your way, do you seek distractions?
  - ❏ I am not feeling good. Let me watch TV or play video games.
  - ❏ Let me tell my friends what happened. They will make me feel better.
  - ❏ Whenever I'm upset, I eat a chocolate. It really uplifts my mood.
  - ❏ I need a break from work. That will help me recover from stress.

- Do your actions and behaviour depend on external factors?
  - ❏ I wanted to speak politely but could not hold back anger when he entered.
  - ❏ I am usually courteous, but with her I just cannot be nice.
  - ❏ Why should I be kind to people who have wronged me?
  - ❏ I don't need to be punctual when my colleagues are always late.

This is certainly not a complete list but you get the idea. How many options did you tick? The higher the number, the greater your emotional dependency.

Let us first attempt to identify our emotional dependencies, although it can be a long list. Some are easier to recognize but many are so subtle that they require a deeper check to be spotted.

External

- **Gadgets and technology**: phone, internet, media, social media, TV
- **Substances**: alcohol, cigarettes, caffeine, prescription and over-the-counter medicine, other legal and illegal drugs
- **Recreation or leisure**: shopping, vacation, movies, gambling
- Food and beverages

Internal

- *Others should behave the way I want them to.*
- *Situations should be to my liking.*
- *I need people to approve of me and appreciate me.*
- *My opinion is right and theirs is wrong.*

Moving From Blame to Accountability

We are often unaware of our emotional dependence. Check the vocabulary of these thoughts and words:

- *He is the cause of my anger.*
- *She hurt me.*
- *I am worried for them.*
- *They are so irritating.*
- *Spending time with you cheers me up.*
- *I am so happy to have bought a new phone.*

These lines clearly reflect our emotional dependence.

- Each time we think or speak this way, we reaffirm that our entire spectrum of emotions—of stress, anger, irritation, happiness, love and so on—is created because of situations, people, places, achievements, positions or objects, and that we have no control over how we feel.
- By believing that our emotions are created by someone or something out there, we are moving away from the truth.

- Each of these sentences carry the negative energy of blame. Such words make us live like victims of circumstances rather than as masters.
- The blame game is dependency, and dependency depletes our inner power. The more we blame, the weaker we become. The weaker we become, the more we believe that the world around us governs our emotions.

A situation or a person's behaviour is an 'external' trigger; it is only a stimulus. Our emotion is our 'internal' creation in response to the stimulus. When every situation is a stimulus, exactly how powerful is this stimulus?

Situations can be challenging. People can be difficult. Someone can exploit, manipulate, cheat, insult or ignore us or they can make mistakes or have wrong habits. They can even cause us physical harm. Read these options again and you will see that they can do all the wrong ONLY OUTSIDE. That is all the power they have. They can NEVER GET INSIDE our minds. They do not have this power. It means they cannot get into our minds and create our thoughts and emotions.

You might say, 'Of course, it is obvious that situations and people cannot get into our minds.'

It is obvious and even children know it. The question then is: when we know this truth, why do we live our life believing that situations and people control our emotions, making us impatient, upset, happy or insecure? Situations are not in our control but our responses are completely in our control. So even if we create stress, anger or hurt, we simply need to remember that no one other than ourselves is to be blamed. Blaming external factors implies giving away our power, believing that they created our turbulent emotions, and so those factors need to change for us to feel fine.

It is important to think this way each time we create any emotion:

- *The situation was tough. I created the stress.*
- *They behaved rudely. I created anger.*
- *He betrayed me. I created all this hurt.*
- *She is manipulative. I created irritation upon watching her behaviour.*

Observe that the vocabulary is of taking personal responsibility for our emotions. Situations may not go our way but our response should always be our way—the right way, the healthy way. That is the only way to experience happiness, health and harmony. Let us internalize: 'I created' is the language or the essence of independence. It means we are choosing our creation. And when we are the creators, we have all the power to change our creation as well, don't we? Let us take a moment to hammer this truth deep into our awareness.

To summarize, follow these simple steps to re-programme your mind and put yourself on the path to emotional independence.

Step 1: Take personal responsibility of your emotions as you enter a scene.

Step 2: Do not justify or endorse a negative emotion, no matter what. Otherwise, you tend to give yourself the liberty to create it again and again. It depletes your inner power.

Step 3: Choose the emotion you wish to experience. You know the list: patience, acceptance, compassion, happiness, love, forgiveness ...

Step 4: Create the emotion you want to experience by creating a corresponding thought.

- In an adverse situation, create this thought: 'I am a peaceful soul. This situation is tough but I am certain about crossing it calmly. I have faith in God, in my ability and in my destiny.'
- If the other person behaves badly, create the thought: 'I am a loving soul. He is behaving badly but I understand he is in emotional pain. I respond with compassion.' You understand them and correct them patiently.

Celebrate Your Freedom

The next time you find a reason to complain about something, create thoughts of gratitude for all the other things going right. If you feel like criticizing someone for a mistake, correct them respectfully rather than angrily. If you feel like worrying about a problem, focus on the solution instead. As you internalize that choosing a healthy response is just one thought away, you will see your responses changing more easily. You will then experience the most powerful form of freedom.

2

The Incredible Power of Your Mind

- *Please calm down.*
- *Don't be scared.*
- *Stop crying.*
- *Why are you so upset?*
- *Come on. That is no reason to feel bad.*

D O YOU RECALL RECEIVING SUCH ADVICE WHILE BEING IN the middle of an emotional outburst? Could you pull yourself together immediately? Or did it take a while to put a lid on your gushing feelings? You had already thought of calming down, hadn't you? But you just did not know how to do it. We have all experienced moments when someone's well-meaning advice seemed unsolicited. It is akin to telling a person who trips and falls, 'You should have walked carefully.' Perhaps no one knows it better than him. After all, he is the one in pain.

Observe Your Mental Space

Reflect on these questions:

- What is the thought on your mind right now?
- Are you thinking about the content you are reading?
- Are you reading the text but are your thoughts somehow drifting towards a completely unrelated topic?
- Are you able to hold your present thought for a few seconds?
- Are you unable to really interpret what you are thinking?

We do not usually observe or recognize our thoughts, but now would be a good time to become aware. Pause, withdraw your attention from your surroundings for twenty seconds and observe what is going on inside your mind. There is always a constant flow of thoughts. Where do you feel them arising? From your heart? Gut? Brain? Or somewhere around the centre of your forehead? It is around the centre of the forehead where thoughts can be felt. Notice that when you overthink or when your thoughts are cluttered, your forehead region feels heavy or aches.

What Are Thoughts?

Thoughts are a conversation or an inner dialogue with our own self. Thoughts are like scripts created by the mind—

naturally, automatically and endlessly. A thought can be an idea, an opinion, a question, an answer and so on. The purpose of a thought is to prompt us to take one or more meaningful actions and create a desired outcome. Every human creation, every discovery and every invention is a consequence of a thought in someone's mind. The mind churns out an unceasing flow of thoughts related to various events, people, ourselves, situations, objects, places … just about anything. Much like every blink, pulse, breath and heartbeat, our thoughts are also incessant.

What You Think Is How You Feel

The mind has two primary functions: the creation of thoughts and the subsequent creation of feelings (emotions). A thought arises in the mind. **A series of thoughts give rise to a feeling.**

Consider these examples of thoughts and the corresponding feelings they generate, in the mind of a person:

Thought	Feeling
I am so grateful I have this home to call mine.	Gratitude
I am happy that my friend bought a lovely home today.	Happiness
This small home helps me stay closer to and bond better with my family.	Love
This house is so small and stuffy.	Dissatisfaction
My friend bought a spacious house which I could not afford.	Jealousy
My colleague is coming home. He may ridicule me for living here.	Worry

The same person is referring to the same house on different occasions. Notice that different thoughts evoke different feelings and emotions. We often pay attention to our feelings rather than to our thoughts. We usually understand and express feelings— that we are feeling low, happy, upset or angry. But we do not pay much attention to our thoughts. We use the word 'thought' only when referring to an idea or opinion. For instance, we say, 'I had a thought', 'I have an idea' or 'I think this is how it works'.

Our feelings are a result of a series of thoughts. If we want to change how we feel, we need to reflect on the quality of thoughts we are creating at the moment, and change them. **Changing our thoughts is the only way to change our feelings.**

Your Experiences, Your Choice

Our thoughts create our experiences. In other words, we experience whatever we think. This means **experiencing feelings like happiness, peace, calmness and cheerfulness is only one thought away.** This is why we should learn to create pure, positive and nice thoughts, irrespective of the situational stimulus. Consider these example scenarios.

Scenario 1

Suppose your colleague and you are headed together for an important business meeting but get stranded in traffic en route. Let us look at a few thoughts that could arise in such a situation. Your colleague says, 'I am afraid we might get late. If the client reaches before us, it will be embarrassing. Besides, our boss will certainly hold it against us.'

His thoughts give him an experience of fear, anxiety, worry and restlessness.

You maintain composure and say: 'Relax. The traffic will clear up and we will reach in time. Everything will be perfect today.'

Your thoughts give you an experience of peace, optimism and faith.

Even if both of you reach the office late and get an earful from your supervisors, your colleague might not have the power to cope since his energy was already spent in worrying. But you will have the energy to face the scene calmly with stability.

Think about this: both of you were in the same situation. If the stimulus was responsible for creating your responses and experiences, then both of you would have created the same thoughts and experienced the same emotions. But that did not happen. It shows that our responses are our choice, regardless of the stimulus.

Scenario 2

Let us reflect on a common scene at home, when a challenging circumstance arises. Each family member thinks and feels differently. One member remarks, 'I am worried about this huge problem'. The second says, 'The problem is not huge. We can overcome it.' The third member quips, 'I do not see any problem. This is just a trivial issue.'

If a stimulus was to create their thoughts, all the three family members would have identical thoughts and feelings. But that is not the case. Someone magnifies a situation through their thoughts. Someone else plays it down with a different kind of thought. This is why different people label situations differently as 'chaos', 'crisis', 'mess', 'problem', 'issue' or 'scenario'. The gravity of any situation depends on how we choose to think about it. Reducing the size of a situation in our mind helps us to overpower it, rather than getting overpowered by it.

Scenario 3

We often meet people who have huge emotional reactions even to a slight cold or a fever. They magnify the illness by creating thoughts like, 'Oh this cold is terrible', 'Fever is tiring me', 'What if I do not recover soon?' On the other hand, we also come across individuals who battle terminal illnesses, remaining emotionally resilient. Their body undergoes extreme suffering but not their mind. They say, 'I have accepted the situation. I will not let it overpower my mind. I want to spend the remaining days joyfully.'

A positive mindset helps us cope better, lowers the sense of pain and distress, increases immunity and even extends life spans in some cases. Many patients make unexpected and spectacular recoveries, defying the predictions of medical science. They prove that health of the body does not create our feelings, but our feelings influence the health of our body.

The three example scenarios prove that situations do not create our responses and experiences. But our responses influence our situations. **It is always—not just sometimes— mind over matter.**

Every Thought Counts

Our thoughts, words, actions and behaviours constitute our karma. The Law of Karma states, 'As will be our karma, so will be our destiny.' Thoughts are the starting point and destiny is where it all culminates. In fact, every thought that the mind creates amounts to our karma. Thus, our mind is not only the space where karma is first created, but it is also where most of our karmas are created, as our thoughts outnumber our words and actions.

Don't we all know individuals who tap into the power of their thoughts to perform feats or achieve goals that are labelled as 'miracles'? They create thoughts of steely determination, faith and power and then act on their thoughts to win against all odds:

- Helen Keller, who lost her vision and hearing before the age of two, was more than just a symbol of courage. She dedicated her life to improving the conditions of those facing hearing and vision impairment through her lectures in over twenty-five countries.
- Dr Stephen Hawking became wheelchair-bound when he was only twenty-one years old. Although his mobility and speech got affected, he went on to become a distinguished scientist, proving that physical disabilities need not become mental barriers.

The Mind and Its Superpower

- Think of a relative who lives in another country.
- Think of your next-door neighbour.
- Think of a vacation you went on, two years ago.
- What was the colour of your school uniform?

How long did it take to think of each of them? Perhaps not more than a second or two. Our mind works at a fast speed and our thoughts also travel quickly. Remaining wherever you are right now, you can radiate a thought to someone who lives on a different continent, because thoughts travel as energy vibrations.

Everything in the universe is energy. This means at every moment, each of us vibrate energetically at a particular frequency. Our vibration refers to the quality of our energy. It is the cumulative result of our intentions, thoughts, feelings, words and actions at any given moment. Just as radio frequencies can be heard but not seen, our vibrations can be felt but not seen. The word 'vibe' is derived from vibrations. When we pay careful attention, we can feel the vibes of another person.

The mind does not have a physical form that we can see or touch, unlike the brain. Note that the mind is separate from the brain, though some people wrongly refer to them interchangeably. The brain is a physical organ, while the mind is more intangible as it is energy. The mind creates a thought and sends a signal to the brain. The brain then brings that thought into action through the body.

Nurture Your Child

- *Mine is a monkey mind, too fickle to stay still.*
- *Controlling my mind is as difficult as controlling the wind.*
- *Mind is like a fast-galloping horse, running absolutely uncontrolled.*

You might have heard someone speak this way about the mind. You might have spoken this way too. But these statements are far from the truth. It is only because we have not paid enough attention to our mind and its workings, that it comes across as being untamed or unruly at times.

Visualize a mother taking care of her infant. Suppose she is alone and needs to complete all the housework as well. She leaves the child in the cradle and goes about her chores. But while doing everything, she frequently checks if her child is playing, sleeping, crying or needs anything. To take care of the child, she does not neglect the house. And to take care of the house, she does not neglect her infant. She is responsible for both, but her child is her first priority, followed by the house. If the child starts crying, she immediately withdraws from her work and goes to her child, tends to the child's needs, consoles the child, and then returns to work.

The mind is like our child; it is the child within. We need to take care of it while taking care of other aspects like home, health, family and career. Our first priority should always be the state of our mind. While going about other tasks, this child—our mind—might start crying, which means it might start feeling irritated, angry, scared, stressed or hurt. Or it might even start questioning, 'Why this, why that, why the other?' At that moment, we need to immediately withdraw from our task for a minute, listen to what the mind is saying, counsel it, silence its chatter and then resume our task.

When a child makes a mistake, we lovingly correct and teach her the right way to do something. The same needs to be done with our mind—this child within is not in our control today only because no one has taught us what to think, how to think or how much to think. We need to parent our mind and teach it about the rights and wrongs. We need to discipline this child with love and assertiveness, rather than using aggression. **Our mind learns whatever it is taught and obediently follows every instruction we give.** Similarly, while dealing with others, let us remember that we are dealing with the child within them.

If we say to ourselves, 'I cannot trust people ever again', our mind, which is listening to us, accepts the statement. Thereafter, before we meet people, our mind starts chattering, 'Do not trust this person. You cannot trust anyone.' But suppose one day we tell our mind, 'Let me trust people. It makes my life easy.' From that day on, we start teaching the child within another way of being. Even if the mind continues doubting people due to past experiences, we just need to patiently remind it, 'No more doubting others. I trust everyone.' Very soon, the mind will learn and follow our instruction.

Can You Ever Stop Thinking?

Whether we are idle, in the middle of an important task, meditating or sleeping, our mind never ceases to think. Did you know that thoughts are created even when a person is in a coma? And even after a soul leaves the body? In other words, there comes a moment when our heart stops beating, the pulse vanishes and our breath comes to a halt. But even then, our mind continues to create thoughts. Do take a moment to appreciate the relentless nature of the mind.

An electroencephalogram (EEG), which has an array of other uses, shows that our mind creates tens of thousands of thoughts in a single day. When the mind is relaxed, peaceful and calm, the number of thoughts come down. When it is stressed, aggressive or anxious, the number of thoughts shoots up. Remember, every thought makes you feel a certain way: comforted, confused, delighted, resentful, fearless … Take another moment to ask yourself: how many out of the thousands of daily thoughts I have are pure, positive and comfortable?

Although emptying the mind and becoming thought-free sounds tempting, it is impossible. The aim should not be to stop thinking but to discipline the mind to think right.

Four Kinds of Thoughts

Knowing that the mind is creating thoughts throughout the day, day after day, year after year, birth after birth, one may wonder if the mind ever feels exhausted. **It is not the quantity but the quality of thoughts that decide if our mind feels fresh or tired.** This is why we need to spend a few minutes every day to observe our thought patterns—of what we think about ourselves and how we think about other people, situations and the world at large. Broadly, our thoughts can be classified into four types: pure, neutral, toxic or wasteful.

1. **Pure thoughts**: These are elevated, positive, powerful and selfless in nature. Pure thoughts are of peace, compassion, love, happiness, forgiveness, gratitude, contentment, kindness and acceptance. They are free from attachments and expectations. They equip us to see the best in every person and situation. We do not question, complain, judge or criticize when our thoughts are pure. Creating pure thoughts does not mean we expect the best to happen at every moment. It just means we accept that whatever happens is accurate for that moment. Thoughts of acceptance keep us stable and empower us to put in our best in the next moment and influence the situation. Also, creating pure thoughts does not imply that we overlook or endorse other people's mistakes. It just means that we do not let our state of mind get affected by them. Pure thoughts enable us to remain stable and then discipline or advise the other person.

   Let us remember that our mind cannot instantly create a series of pure thoughts when a challenging situation arises. Such thoughts result from consistent and systematic practice.

2. **Neutral thoughts**: These are thoughts pertaining to our activities or actions, ranging from the mundane to the sophisticated. They often relate to our roles and responsibilities in personal and professional life. Examples of neutral thoughts are, 'I need to do this', 'What is her phone number?' or 'He will meet me next week.' These thoughts are neutral since we are neither creating positive nor negative energy through them, which means we are neither energizing our inner power nor depleting it.

But often, in a subtle and unaware way, we pile up negative and wasteful thoughts as a follow-up to neutral thoughts. For instance, 'It is time for breakfast' is a neutral thought. But we often follow it up with thoughts like, 'Why is it not ready on time?', 'The dining table is also not set', 'Don't they know their job even after all these years?', 'No matter how much I explain, they will never understand.' In this series of thoughts, there is only one neutral thought, which is, 'It is time for breakfast.' The remaining are either negative or wasteful.

3. **Toxic thoughts**: These are clearly harmful as they take away our peace and stability. Thoughts of ego, anger, greed, hatred, fear, criticism, disagreement, laziness, bias, jealousy and stress are toxic or negative. Such thoughts are driven by selfish motives and expectations, so creating them neither benefits the situation nor the people involved. The mind is habituated to creating several toxic thoughts, as soon as a situation is not favourable. If we do not pause and change the toxic thoughts created in one scene, we tend to carry the emotional disturbance into a subsequent scene, and turn that also into a negative experience. This cascading effect causes our mind to accumulate negative thoughts and emotions. Over prolonged periods, they harm our emotional, mental and physical health, and our relationships.

4. **Wasteful thoughts**: Carrying no constructive purpose, these thoughts are exactly what they are labelled: wasteful. We often spend unreasonable amounts of

time thinking, 'Why did he have to do that?', 'What if I do not get admission in that university?' or 'Look at how she behaves'. When we get into the why, where, when and how of things which are not in our control, our mind starts creating a series of wasteful thoughts. These thoughts dwell on the events we can do nothing about, like ruminating or reminiscing about the past, and anticipating or worrying about the future. Even deliberating other people's behaviour and forming opinions about things not concerning us are wasteful thoughts. They might seem harmless, but they are silently harming us by tiring the mind and wasting our limited time and energy. Whether we had to face hardship at work, someone betrayed us or a relationship failed, the incident has already happened and we cannot do anything about it now.

Research shows that 85 per cent of our daily thoughts are wasteful. We can do the math: of the remaining 15 per cent, what is the percentage of negative and neutral thoughts? And how small is the percentage of pure thoughts?

Creating one negative or wasteful thought after another depletes our mental energy reserves. This is why we feel mentally tired or fatigued, even when leading physically comfortable lives. But our mind which creates over 85 per cent of wrong thoughts, is perfectly capable of creating 100 per cent pure and elevated thoughts. That is our potential. And that is the journey of soul strengthening that we have embarked on.

3

Shape Your Life One Thought at a Time

Y OU WALK INTO A SHOWROOM TO BUY A SMARTPHONE and say to the saleswoman, 'All I am looking for is a simple phone only for calls and messages'. She shows you a new model and you instantly like it. She starts demonstrating how to use it, but you stop her and say, 'That is all right. I will figure it out eventually. Just pack it.' You are happy about the purchase. All is well until a month later, when the phone freezes and you have no idea what to do. You panic and rush to the showroom, where you give that saleswoman an earful. She inspects the phone, restarts it and then it works like a charm. You wish you had learnt a thing or two about it, especially when she had offered to teach. That would have saved your energy and time.

This applies to how some of us live. When life is going smoothly, we do not pay attention to the several aspects working in our favour. But on the day something goes wrong, it is a different story altogether. We struggle to deal with that obstacle, failure or setback. We start panicking and remain clueless about the solution. We go to other people for help and support.

In this book we are trying to analyse why life is the way it is. Making inroads into the world behind our eyebrows, we are now aware that our inner world of beliefs, thoughts, feelings, actions and karmas are connected to our outer world of achievements, possessions, roles and relationships.

The Inside Story

There is an extremely subtle and invisible mechanism within each of us that guides us to think, feel, speak, behave and respond in certain ways. These inner workings are responsible for how our life pans out—our past, present and future. They determine what happens to us at every moment.

Our life follows a very powerful and constant internal process flow, which goes like this:

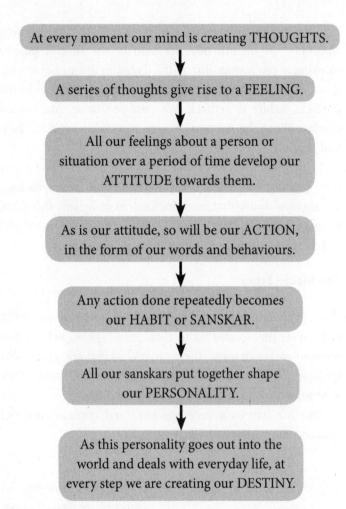

At every moment our mind is creating THOUGHTS.

A series of thoughts give rise to a FEELING.

All our feelings about a person or situation over a period of time develop our ATTITUDE towards them.

As is our attitude, so will be our ACTION, in the form of our words and behaviours.

Any action done repeatedly becomes our HABIT or SANSKAR.

All our sanskars put together shape our PERSONALITY.

As this personality goes out into the world and deals with everyday life, at every step we are creating our DESTINY.

Starting with our thoughts, notice how all the elements listed above are connected all the way to our destiny. Working in tandem, each stage has a cascading effect that creates a flow:

Thoughts – Feelings – Attitude – Action – Habit/Sanskar – Personality – Destiny

It All Begins with a Thought

Thoughts – Feelings – Attitude – Action – Habit/Sanskar –
Personality – Destiny

'**I am the creator of my thoughts. I choose them, I create them**'—we need to keep reminding ourselves of this time and time again. We need to embed this truth so deep into our awareness that we practically experience the thought creation process in every scene of life.

In response to the same situations, different people create different thoughts. The situation does not create our thought; we create our thoughts in response to the stimulus or situation. Suppose a family member needs financial help and you lend her money. You have different choices of what to think while helping her. One option is to think, 'Just because I am wealthy, everyone wants me to help her.' This thought is not a good one. Instead, you can create a better thought, such as, 'I am happy to be of help. My blessings are always with her. I am certain she will overcome her problems and reach her goal.'

Can you see the difference? In the first case, the situation overpowers your state of mind and as a consequence, influences your thoughts and feelings. In the second case, your mind becomes more powerful than the situation. In either case, however, you are the creator of the thought, not the situation. Applying this powerful realization transforms us from victims to masters of our circumstances and lives.

We are not called 'human doings' although we are constantly engaged in 'doing' one thing after another for an entire lifetime. We are called 'human beings' because we are a 'being' who influences the 'doing'. We are not a 'doing' who influences the 'being'. Every morning, we mentally organize our thoughts by asking ourselves, 'What should I do today?' Now, we just need to add another dimension to this: 'How should I be?'

Let us start creating thoughts of how we will be while doing any activity—while we get ready for office, when in traffic, while we work on projects or chair a team meeting, when we return home and spend time with our family. For instance, if you have a meeting to chair, think and visualize how you are going to BE in the meeting while executing your list of things to DO: 'I remain calm, I listen patiently, I state my views respectfully, I stand for what is right, I empower others to think right.'

Thoughts Trigger Feelings

Thoughts – **Feelings** – Attitude – Action – Habit/Sanskar – Personality – Destiny

Thoughts are our creations. A series of thoughts give rise to our feelings or emotions—happiness is a feeling, peace is a feeling, love is a feeling. These are feelings we experience because of the thoughts we create.

We succeed at times, fail at other times; people obey us at times, disobey us at other times; we receive compliments at times, criticism at other times; we are healthy at times, we feel aches or pain at other times. That is certain. When we do not focus on our inner world, how we feel becomes dependent on our outer circumstances, and hence our feelings start to fluctuate. If a situation is favourable, we feel great. Otherwise, we become overwhelmed by pain, anxiety, irritation, anger or fear. We are often aware of our feelings but not of our thoughts. Sometimes, we want to change how we feel, but are unable to do so because feelings are created as an outcome of thoughts. All we need to do is reflect on the kind of thoughts we have been creating and change those thoughts. **It is impossible to change our feelings without changing our thoughts.** Consider two examples to understand how feelings are connected to thoughts:

- Create a thought: 'Let me eat my favourite chocolate.' Notice how this thought makes you feel pleased, assuming you like chocolates.

  When unwrapping the chocolate bar, suppose you think, 'It is generous of my friend to gift me a whole box of chocolates.' This thought makes you feel grateful and cared for.

  As you eat it, suppose you create a thought, 'Delicious! It has just the right amount of cocoa.' This thought triggers happiness and satisfaction.

  Next, if you think, 'Let me hide it. I do not want anyone else to eat them,' you will experience uncomfortable feelings of greed and insecurity.

- Recall an argument you had with a friend. Now, create a thought: 'She was wrong and she was too egoistic to admit her mistake.' You feel angry and upset.

  Then, if you think, 'I did the right thing by proving her wrong. Now everyone knows I am innocent.' These thoughts make you feel delighted and satisfied.

  If you continue thinking, 'But I did not like how it ended. Our friendship of two years ended bitterly. Maybe I was rude.' You can see how these thoughts make you feel unhappy and guilty.

In both scenarios, examine how your different thoughts generate different feelings and emotions.

Can Distractions Help You Heal?

You might ask, 'When I can simply distract my mind to cope with negative and uncomfortable feelings, why should I make the effort to change my thoughts?' Let us use an example to understand why this will not work.

A person headed to a movie theatre slips and falls, hurting his knee. The wound obviously hurts but he thinks, 'I am already late to the theatre. I am sure the movie will divert my mind from this pain.' Sure enough, his attention is distracted for the next three hours. After the movie ends, he senses pain again. He thinks, 'Wow! I had forgotten about this wound. Let me spend some time with friends. I will feel better.' The wounded knee occasionally bothers him, but he continues to ignore it. By end of the day, while walking home, he finds the pain too sharp to bear. He examines the injury and finds a significant increase in swelling and redness. He regrets not attending to it earlier.

Many of us deal with emotional wounds in a similar way. By end of the day, sometimes there is a lot on our mind— thoughts and feelings of stress, fatigue, anger, dissatisfaction, anxiety and so on. But instead of healing them, we prefer to run away from our mind's negative inner chatter. We distract the mind so that, somehow, we start feeling better. Today we have so many distractions at our disposal that we easily shift from one to the next. We seek relief and relaxation mostly through the phone, television, parties, shopping, books, holidays, substance addictions and so on. This is a good juncture for self-reflection:

❏ When did you last sit with yourself for 15 minutes,
   doing nothing?
❏ Are you comfortable in your own company without
   the need to reach for your phone, the TV remote
   control or a book?
❏ When you are alone, do you feel lonely?

Being with yourself means being comfortable with the
thoughts and feelings in your mind. When you are feeling
relaxed, calm and peaceful, you will easily be able to sit
with yourself. In those moments you can be alone but never
lonely, because you will enjoy being in the company of your
clean mind and pure vibrations. Oftentimes, we uplift a
close friend's mood and they lift ours. Now, we need to do
that with ourselves because our goal is to achieve emotional
independence. Self-counselling is a valuable skill to master,
and these are simple steps to do it:

Step 1: Write your thoughts about the issue on your mind.

Step 2: Answer those thoughts as if you were consoling someone
else—with patience, love and empathy.

Step 3: You may have to repeat this a few times because at times
the mind keeps going back and forth and needs time to heal.

Distractions do not heal. Even time does not heal. It is we
who create our emotional wounds. So it is we who need to heal
them. **An emotional wound is caused by wrong thoughts.**

It can be healed with a right thought. For instance, 'I am good for nothing' is a thought that hurts. 'I am a powerful soul who can do anything I decide to' is a thought that heals.

Feelings Develop Your Attitude

Thoughts – Feelings – **Attitude** – Action – Habit/Sanskar – Personality – Destiny

Do you see a glass as half full or half empty? This question can be a good starting point for an attitude check. 'Attitude means everything' is a popular saying for a reason. If there is one aspect of our personality which instantly reflects in all our relationships, friendships, work or health, it is our attitude. **Attitude is a mental filter through which we perceive and experience the world.** It is developed based on how we feel about ourselves, other people, objects, events and situations in life. Our attitude is created by our feelings, which in turn are created by our thoughts. So, our attitude does not just 'come' to us. It is our creation and it affects every dimension of our life.

People are who they are and situations are how they should be. Feeling a certain way for the same people and situations over a period of time develops our attitude towards them. So, our attitude decides whether we accept, reject, respect or disrespect people and situations. There is a wide spectrum of healthy and unhealthy attitudes that all of us carry—friendly, arrogant, pleasant, indifferent, grateful, selfish and so on. Consider these examples:

- *I am certain that the team will perform well under him.* (Optimistic attitude)

- *When you become fearless, life becomes limitless.* (Fearless, ambitious attitude)
- *My door is open to anyone who needs help.* (Caring and kind attitude)
- *I cannot stand people who behave like they are always right.* (Dismissive attitude)
- *That is just how I am. You take it or leave it.* (Arrogant attitude)
- *I ordered chocolate flavour but they served vanilla. I ate without making a fuss.* (Easy-going attitude)

Our attitude impacts the quality of our life way more deeply than we realize. A positive, healthy attitude boosts our character and energy. It acts as a magnet to attract more success and wellbeing into our life. Even in the face of a failure or setback, a positive attitude enables us to learn, see possibilities and solutions and bounce back. It motivates us to reaffirm that every situation is accurate and beneficial. It becomes a tool to overcome obstacles and accomplish our goals. It also equips us to evolve into a stronger individual.

In contrast, having a negative attitude makes us perceive everything with pessimism; that if something can go wrong in life, it certainly will. We tend to focus on what is not right in people, situations or events and overlook the good. Instead of spotting possibilities, we spot limitations. We often feel annoyed, become disrespectful and hostile towards people and situations. Every challenge becomes a stumbling block and at times we tend to give up on ourselves and others. Unhealthy attitude blocks our peace, happiness, love and blessings. As an inevitable result, we attract more pain and misery.

Attitude Determines Your Action

Thoughts – Feelings – Attitude – **Action** – Habit/Sanskar – Personality – Destiny

Our behaviour at times seems too complex to predict, understand or explain. However, attitude is a key predictor of actions or behaviour. It is proven to have a strong bearing on what we say or do. In other words, **our actions are an outward or visible expression of our attitude**. It is our attitude which comes out as the words we speak, the actions we take, the way we conduct ourselves and the behaviours we exhibit. The stronger our attitude, the more likely that it affects our actions, behaviour or response to people, objects, events and situations. For instance, consider someone who has a healthy attitude towards his career. This attitude makes him proactive, efficient and sincere at work. It reflects in his behaviour with co-workers—he understands, cooperates, shares and cares. His impeccable work ethic inspires others to give their best. On the contrary, an employee who carries an unhealthy attitude will eventually display inefficiency, indifference and discontentment. His negative attitude leads to behavioural issues like arrogance, carelessness and manipulation. He eventually becomes a liability to the organization.

Repeated Actions Form Your Habits and Sanskars

Thoughts – Feelings – Attitude – Action – **Habit/Sanskar** –
Personality – Destiny

Any action done repeatedly becomes a sanskar. A sanskar is similar to a habit. Habits refer to physical activities while sanskars refer to emotional patterns. For instance, eating, walking and sleeping are habits. Caring, accepting and complaining are sanskars.

Suppose you get a new job and you reach office on time every day. Within a few days, punctuality becomes your sanskar. But for over a month, you notice that most of your colleagues arrive almost thirty minutes late. This sets you thinking, 'No one appreciates and no one even knows that I come on time daily. So there is no point abiding by office timings. Why should I alone be punctual? Let me also start coming late.' You feel uncomfortable about making this choice, but nevertheless stick to it. Within a few days, coming late becomes your sanskar, overriding your previous sanskar of punctuality.

Reflect on how your thoughts eventually give rise to sanskars. **Changing a sanskar is just one thought away.** It is also important to note that our sanskars often change for the better too. Someone who is a habitual latecomer might start valuing her and other people's time. She therefore creates a sanskar of punctuality.

Sanskars Define Your Personality

Thoughts – Feelings – Attitude – Action – Habit/Sanskar –
Personality – Destiny

- *Which three words best describe you?*
- *Tell us something about yourself.*
- *What are your strengths and weaknesses?*

Have you been asked such questions, especially during an interview? Sometimes we find it challenging as we may not even know the answer. This is because many of us have not made the effort to know or understand ourselves.

Take this moment to introspect: 'What is my personality? What personality would I like to have?'

All our sanskars and habits combined together shape our personality. Personality is 'inside' of us. It is a cumulative result of our thoughts, feelings, memories, attitude, actions and habits.

All of us like perfection as that is our original nature. We tend to focus on perfection in what we do and in how we look. There is a lot of focus today on cosmetic enhancements to create a perfect face. Let us also focus on perfection in the aspects that matter most: intentions, thoughts, feelings, behaviours and vibrations. Having an imperfect mind but trying to create a perfect face will not give us the perfection we desire. Someone who undergoes cosmetic treatment to enhance her smile may not necessarily be happy within. What energy will she radiate? When we are the same on the inside and the outside, which means when our words and behaviours are aligned with our feelings, then our energies are in harmony. We thereby radiate purity and simplicity.

Personality implies the person—who we are or what our characteristics are. **Sanskars, which means personality traits, serve as the building blocks of personality.** Personality is like a whole package made of different sanskars. For instance, we could say, 'I am resilient', 'I am optimistic', 'I am loyal', 'I am humble', 'I am arrogant', 'I am creative'. Each one of these characteristics make up our underlying personality traits or sanskars. They come together to shape who we are as a person. There can also be negative shades to our personality such as domination, manipulation, stubbornness, immaturity or intolerance.

Personality is also subject to change because our sanskars keep changing from time to time. So regardless of how it is now, our personality can be groomed and evolved. A good example is of students whose personalities get deeply influenced during their stay at a hostel. Consider a student who has a controlling personality living with a roommate who has a humble personality. Over a period, the dominating student realizes that his roommate has an admirable personality and decides to become like the latter. That student makes conscious efforts to change his way of thinking and speaking, and even his behaviour and mannerisms. He creates a sanskar of humility. When his sanskars start changing, his personality also starts changing for good.

Personality in Action Manifests Your Destiny

Thoughts – Feelings – Attitude – Action – Habit/Sanskar –
Personality – **Destiny**

We are actors performing in the drama of life, and this world is like an enormous stage. The personality of the actor will reflect in every role and scene. We have seen that our personality is a collection of our thoughts, words, attitude, actions, behaviours, habits and sanskars. Our personality stays with us constantly, whether we are at home, at work, at a social gathering or at a spiritual organization. It radiates energy from us to the world at every moment. As is the energy we send out, so will be the energy we receive. Our every thought, word and behaviour is the energy we create and send out. That is our karma. According to the Law of Karma, the energy we receive in return as a consequence, is our destiny. As is our karma, so will be the consequence of the karma. Remember this:

- Your every **thought** is a karma that influences your destiny.
- Your every **word** is a karma that influences your destiny.
- Your every **behaviour** is a karma that influences your destiny.

Be the Captain of Your Ship

If life is comparable to a voyage, we are the captains of our ships. On some days, sailing towards our goal is smooth. On other days, we need to battle rough storms or the turbulent winds of challenges. As skilful captains, we need to use our resources of pure intentions, energizing thoughts and empowering words to keep our ships afloat and steer them to safety.

Ultimately, your destiny depends only on your thoughts.

4

Why You Think the Way You Think

- *My thoughts seem to come from nowhere.*
- *I do not choose what to think. Thoughts occur by themselves.*
- *Thoughts do not mean much to me. They just come and go.*
- *Thoughts arise from the brain ... or the heart.*

ARE YOU FAMILIAR WITH SUCH STATEMENTS? HAVING visited the engine room of our inner world, we have learnt that thoughts are created in our mind, and that our every thought is our own choice. We have also understood that changing our thoughts changes our destiny. But for us to change our thoughts, we need to be aware of the very basis of thought creation. What are the raw materials available for our mind to create thoughts?

The Three Doorways to Your Thoughts

Have you wondered how someone is able to think positively in the toughest of situations, while someone else thinks negatively even in a perfect scenario? Why do our minds work so differently? The difference is caused by these three sources, which our mind uses to create thoughts:

1. The **beliefs** we hold
2. The **content** we consume
3. The **past experiences** we carry

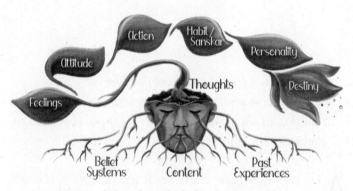

Sources of Thoughts, which then lead up to Destiny

To gain more control over our thought patterns, let us check how these three sources influence our mind. Then it becomes easy to know the root cause for either purity or toxicity in our thoughts.

Source 1: The Beliefs You Hold

A belief is an idea that we hold and consider to be the truth. Our ability to think and reason leads us to believe some things and disbelieve other things based on experiments, experiences and conditioning. Consciously or unconsciously, we have gathered thousands of beliefs across nearly every aspect of life. All our beliefs are ingrained in the subconscious mind. On the basis of these beliefs, thoughts are created in the conscious layer of our mind.

Examples of a few beliefs we might be holding are:

- *I am too thin.*
- *She is the best person in the world.*
- *People are so rude these days.*
- *Life is a competition.*
- *Stress is normal.*
- *Expectations are natural.*
- *Gratitude is the best attitude.*
- *The world is no longer a nice place.*

It is important to be aware of our belief systems because beliefs lead us all the way to our destiny. Take a few minutes to write what you believe about yourself, your body, your family, your life and the world around you. Thereafter, you can keep adding to the list.

The mind assumes that our beliefs are the absolute truth. We become convinced about them even if certain beliefs make us uncomfortable. We gather many layers of beliefs, particularly during our formative years. Show a two-year-old a chair and tell him it is a table. He will 'believe' it to be a table. But for how long will he continue to do that? Perhaps until someone else corrects him or maybe until he learns at school that it is a chair. That day, he will change his belief about that piece of furniture. This is a simple example but the same logic applies even to the profound beliefs we hold. For instance, tell a young child that she is no good. She will believe it until someone shows her how capable she is. **It is important to note that we do change our beliefs from time to time.**

When Labels Become Beliefs

Whenever you think of a relative, friend or colleague, do you associate that person with labels such as arrogant, timid, dishonest, weak, wise and so on? Our perceptions about certain people leads us to create either positive or negative labels for them. These labels then become the mental filter or lens through which we see them.

The risk of labelling someone is that, more often than not, they start viewing themselves through those labels. They embrace our beliefs about who they are. This means labels become beliefs. As a result, they then start living by the labels they receive. The vibrations of labels we give, radiate to them and trigger more of that particular behaviour or habit in them. For instance, if we repeatedly label people as dishonest, we reinforce the sanskar of dishonesty in them. When this label becomes their belief, it impacts their thoughts and thereby their destiny. We therefore become instrumental in altering that person's destiny in a negative way. Without realizing this, we say, 'I just spoke the truth. That person is indeed dishonest.'

When we perceive people through the labels we attribute to them, eventually, we draw the vibrations of that label into our own energy field. Everyone has admirable qualities. Focusing on them, magnifying them and attributing positive labels to the person who displays these qualities will uplift other people and elevate our thinking as well. But by labelling people negatively, we lower our vibrations and disempower them. Therefore, it is important to take care of what we believe about others, especially children, and how we label them.

Children who learn everything about the world from parents, teachers and other elders, also learn about themselves from these people. Here are examples of common labels assigned to children:

- *You are a troublemaker.*
- *Why are you so cranky all the time?*
- *Stop being such a cry-baby.*
- *My son is too picky.*
- *You are extremely talented.*
- *My children are athletic.*
- *My students are brilliant.*
- *You are always sincere.*
- *My son is humble.*

You might ask: 'If a child is fussy, what else should I label him?' The golden rule is: do not create a label for who they are, create a label for who you want them to be. Don't we know about parents and teachers creating miracles with children, simply by reinforcing positive labels?

- A mother received a complaint that her five-year-old son does not speak to anyone in the class. Instead of asking, 'Why are you introverted?', she lovingly said to her son with belief and conviction, 'You are so friendly that your classmates want to talk to you. It is perfectly fine that you were quiet today. Tomorrow, show them your new lunchbox and share your meal with everyone. I will pack extra food.' She consciously kept labelling her son as friendly, cordial and sociable in her thoughts and words. Within a week, her son made two friends.

- A teacher observed that her student was particularly lazy, and decided to change her approach. She said to him, 'You are so diligent. From today you will be the class representative. I am sure you will enjoy the additional responsibilities.' Believing in his abilities, she motivated him daily with labels such as agile, active, enthusiastic, quick and lively. She even gave him appreciation stickers in front of his classmates. The student did not even realize how soon he overcame laziness.

The next time you find yourself judging other people, pause and tell yourself, 'I believe everyone is pure and powerful. I apply only empowering labels on them.'

Have you been given negative labels by people around you? Do you choose to label yourself as who you are—or are not—based on your appearance, background, personality or achievements? Just as people see us through their perceptions, we also see ourselves through certain labels that we put on the self. Remember, they are just labels that reflect a belief. Even if a negative label has become your belief system and a part of your personality, it is just a belief. And a belief can be changed.

Our labels affect our destiny. Let us replace every single negative label we have on ourselves with a pure, powerful and positive label. Let us make them a part of our vocabulary and repeat them consistently for a few days until those positive labels become our identity. To create the reality you want, begin with assigning only the highest energy labels to yourself. Choose the labels of who you want to be in reality. Here are a few labels you can apply on yourself:

- *I am always calm.*
- *I am always respectful.*
- *I do whatever I decide to do.*
- *I complete all my tasks before time.*
- *I am perfect in everything I do.*
- *I am always successful.*

Remind yourself, 'I label myself only and only with positive words. I am aware that my labels are my belief systems which manifest my destiny.'

Take a moment to change at least one negative belief about yourself.

Evaluate Your Beliefs

We are entitled to have beliefs we want, about ourselves, about the people in our life, about our circumstances or about the world. It is our prerogative. However, it is important to believe what is right, what is true and what is healthy. Consider the belief, 'A good diet, exercise and sleep are the pillars of wellbeing.' When the mind believes this, it creates thoughts such as:

- *Let me eat for health and not for taste.*
- *I will not miss my regular exercises.*
- *I should get adequate and good-quality sleep each night.*

But if we hold on to the belief, 'Eat, drink and be merry,' our thoughts will be along the lines of:

- *Just offer me pizza and fries, and I will eat them instantly.*
- *I have no time for a workout.*
- *Let me sacrifice sleep and enjoy binge-watching my favourite show tonight.*

We transmit our belief systems to people around us—especially to family, colleagues and friends. Our belief system can become the belief system of others because of three reasons:

- We live our life through that belief, so they start embracing it.
- We advise or try to convince people that it is right.
- We repeatedly radiate the vibration of that belief to people through our thoughts, words and behaviour, so they get influenced to accept it.

It is important to check whether our beliefs allow us to remain happy, healthy and loving. Sometimes, we don't like our beliefs being challenged. But it helps to re-evaluate if our beliefs are empowering or depleting us.

Let a belief system just remain a belief and not your truth until you experiment with it. To know if a particular belief is right, check if it conforms to these four criteria. Ask yourself:

> - *Does this belief make me emotionally stronger?*
> - *Does it make me mentally and physically healthier?*
> - *Is it creating harmony in my relationships?*
> - *Is it making my life simpler?*
>
> If these four criteria are fulfilled, the belief is comfortable and worth its weight in gold. You can hold on to it as the truth.

Beliefs Requiring Course Correction

Consider these opposite pairs of beliefs. In each case, check if your belief matches Option 1 or 2.

	Option 1	Option 2
1.	*Situations affect my state of mind.*	*I create my thoughts in response to situations.*
2.	*Everything happens as per Gods will.*	*My karmas create my destiny.*
3.	*I will be happy when I reach my goal.*	*I am happy while working towards my goal.*
4.	*Stress is normal.*	*Pressures are normal, I face them with ease.*
5.	*Happiness can be bought.*	*Comforts are bought. Happiness is a state of mind.*
6.	*I need love.*	*I am love. I radiate love.*

	Option 1	Option 2
7.	*Anger is necessary.*	*Compassion and empathy are necessary.*
8.	*Expectations from people are natural.*	*Accepting people is natural.*
9.	*Values do not work in todays world.*	*Values work every single time.*
10.	*It is the nature of the mind to be fickle.*	*The mind can be disciplined to remain stable.*

Let us evaluate two of the beliefs listed in the above table. You may thereafter analyse the others and embrace the right belief.

- **Belief 1**
  Option 1: Situations affect my state of mind.
  Today, external situations are more uncertain than ever. If we make our state of mind dependent on them, then our reactions also become uncertain. Wasteful thoughts will be created, such as, 'How can I be at peace when this situation is not favourable?', 'I fear losing my job or taking a pay cut' or 'The weather is so depressing'. Questioning why, where, when or how will make us live a life of dependency, blame and vulnerability.

  Option 2: I create my thoughts in response to situations.
  External situations are only a stimulus. Our response is always our choice. Whatever the present moment contains, we have the power to accept it and shift our focus from the problem towards a solution. Our response depends on

who we are, our nature and our personality. We need to detach ourselves from the energy of the situation, connect to our inner self and choose a response that benefits everyone involved in that situation.

- **Belief 2**
  Option 1: I will be happy when I reach my goal.
  Whether it is grades, qualifications, designation or status—our goals give us direction. But if we tie happiness to goals, we will say, 'I will be happy when I achieve this'. If we postpone our happiness to an imaginary point in the future when a desire will be fulfilled, we will give ourselves the permission to create other feelings—stress, anger, fear, insecurity, jealousy—until we reach the goal.
  Option 2: I am happy working towards my goal.
  This belief helps us to know that happiness is not dependent on anything outside, but is a conscious choice we make. Happiness then becomes the way we respond to every situation that comes in the way of reaching our goal. **We realize that goals are in our 'doing', while the 'being' (self) experiences happiness along the journey.**

Your past experiences or the beliefs of other people might suggest that Option 1 often seems to be the norm in all the example scenarios. But if you experiment with Option 2, you might realize they are right. To be sure, pass each option through the four criteria discussed earlier: does it make you emotionally stronger, mentally and physically healthier, create harmony in relationships and make life simpler?

Continue to experiment with Option 2 for a few more days. If it still feels right, that belief gradually becomes stronger and gets ingrained in your way of living. A belief remains an abstract concept until we experiment with it. Only when we experience a favourable result does a belief become the truth for us.

Source 2: The Content You Consume

The information or content we feed into the mind constitutes the second source for the generation of our thoughts. Every piece of information we consume, whether important or not and whether we pay attention to it or not, becomes a source for our thoughts. This means everything that we hear, watch, read, write and converse about is information for the mind. It is our emotional diet. Once it is taken in, the information gets absorbed in the mind. It becomes our vibration, our energy—just like the food we eat becomes our nutrition, the energy of the body.

Suppose your child does not return from school at the usual time and her friends do not know her whereabouts. What thoughts come to your mind? Are they thoughts of calmness and faith, such as these?

- *She might be talking to friends and has forgotten to call me.*
- *I am sure she is in the library working on her new project.*
- *Her bicycle might have broken down. I am sure she is fine.*
- *God's blessings of protection are with her. She will be home any moment now.*

Congratulations if your thought pattern is along the lines of optimism. It means while you make efforts to check on your child's wellbeing, internally you remain powerful and stable. Unfortunately, most parents tend to create thoughts of fear and anxiety similar to these:

- *What if my child is involved in an accident?*
- *I was too harsh yesterday when she told me about her grades. Is she scared to come home?*
- *There are so many cases of child abduction these days ... I am so worried.*
- *I know it is not permitted, but maybe I should give her a mobile phone.*

The mind is drawn into negativity quickly, believing it to be normal. As is often the case, your child returns home safely. Even though you are relieved to see her, chances are you do not remain calm. Your temperament and harsh words lead to arguments. If you reflect on the incident later, your mind thinks of the reason for the arguments and blames the child. Actually, your child is not at fault; rather, it is the fault of your pent-up negative thoughts created while waiting for her.

Do you pause to ask yourself why negative thoughts came so naturally to you and what is influencing your response to scenes of daily life? Although we know it is not right, we often think negatively or react impulsively because of the influence of the information we consume.

Ask yourself: how much information do I consume per day?

Assuming you sleep for eight hours a day, it means you are awake for sixteen hours. When you are awake, your mind is constantly fed with information since you engage in activities like hearing, watching, speaking, or reading. This translates to approximately sixteen hours or 66 per cent of your waking hours a day being spent in consuming information. So you are continuously either creating information or consuming it.

Today, there is no end to the information served to us. There is always another notification on the phone to clear, another news headline to catch up on TV, another tweet to read, another post to like, another email to answer, etc. While it gives us an illusion of being well-informed, we are only wasting time endlessly trying to keep up with the deluge of data.

Curation Is the Key

Pure, positive and good news far outweigh the negative incidents occurring across the world. Useful and encouraging content is always available, but not everything can be reported. It is not possible to have a news headline reading 'Over 5 million people reached home safely after work yesterday'. Whereas 'five arrested, three abduction cases solved' is reported and rightly so. The negative energy of such information gets imprinted in people's minds and is largely the reason for parents to readily think of an accident or abduction when children do not return on time.

Even in the name of entertainment, the quality of content we consume has become questionable. If we are consuming content which has ego, lust, greed, aggression, fear, hatred and other such negative emotions, then it is natural for these vibrations to dictate the quality of our thoughts. Choosing the content you consume is as important as choosing what you eat, if not more. Be aware and make informed choices. **Not knowing something may not necessarily equate to ignorance. But knowing what to know is wisdom.**

For those of us who grew up in an era when the first TV, the first computer and the first phone made their way into our homes, our content consumption was minimal. Until then we were entertained or informed just by books from the school or college library, the newspaper and the conversations we picked up from adults at home. Look at how technology has overpowered our lives only because we have become enslaved to it, instead of controlling it:

- Back in the day, there were fewer television channels. TV shows aired just one episode of a show per week. Today, with streaming services and over-the-top platforms, people can choose what to watch and when. This has led to a rise in binge-watching.

- In the past, cell phones were used only for calls and text messages. Today, they have become an indispensable part of life. Checking notifications every other minute has led to overuse and distracts us from important tasks. It has been acknowledged that several applications on the phone are designed to manipulate our mind—to entice us and keep us hooked.

- Social media platforms were created to connect us. But most of us are using them to seek social validation. We post a message and wait patiently (or impatiently) for people to notice, like and approve of it. More 'likes' make us feel worthy. Otherwise, we suffer from low self-esteem.

Many of us do not sleep on time because we want to catch up on a favourite show online. We do not eat right because of surfing TV channels at mealtimes. We deprive ourselves of rest because of mindless scrolling. We do not spend time with our family because we are busy liking and commenting on social media posts. Indulgence in media and social media is aggravating our sanskars of aggression, jealousy, worry, fear, criticism, hatred, comparison and competition. We then respond to scenes of life through these sanskars. Can you see the correlation between content and your wellbeing? Can you see how content is affecting your happiness, health and relationships? In the last twenty years, we have created a world where diabetes, depression, cancer and divorce have become common. Content has a huge role to play in all this.

Let us internalize:
Content = Thoughts = Destiny

Curate the content you consume so as to avoid any negative information that can lead to thoughts of stress, worry, anxiety, aggression or fear. More importantly, carry a book containing empowering messages or save positive messages and talks on your phone. The moment you feel disturbed or low, immediately read or listen to them. Even a five-minute intake of elevated information stops the series of negative thoughts. The message might even give you a solution. This instant nourishment strengthens the soul and gives you the power to create a positive response. It can act as your emotional first-aid kit.

Source 3: The Past Experiences You Carry

The third source for our thoughts is our bundle of past experiences and memories. Rewind your memory slightly and replay the scenes of the last few days on the screen of your mind. A lot must have happened. Most scenes would perhaps be beautiful, pleasant and worthwhile. There could also be an experience you wish to put aside. Did someone not behave rightly with you? Did you carry it in your mind when you went to sleep that night? Reflect if you told yourself, 'What was the need for him to be so rude? He could have said it softly instead of creating such a scene. I should not have kept quiet. I should have retaliated.'

What you did just now is that you consciously went into the past. Was it useful? No, because the painful memory disturbed your peaceful mind. Oftentimes, when in the middle of a task or even when we are idle, several memories flood our mind. And then we rewind all the more to recall all aspects of each memory—what happened, where it happened, who were involved, what they did, how we responded. We also wish that some things should have panned out differently. Usually, an unreasonable duration of time elapses before we realize we were lost in our thoughts and return to the present. The incident is long over but we are unnecessarily reliving it. Just as everything has its place, the past also has one—it belongs in the past.

Drop Your Emotional Baggage

- *My parents love my sister more. They celebrated her fifth birthday but not mine.*

- *My friend hated that I was possessive about her. I should have been careful.*
- *I will never forget the humiliation I faced during the university admission interview.*

Who we were, what we did, our successes, our failures, our strengths and our weaknesses have all together shaped us into who we are today. Our subconscious mind is like a bank or cupboard that has stocked up every single memory as a recording or impression, second by second as it all happened. These memories are used by our conscious mind as the input to create thoughts. It might be fine to open our mental cupboard occasionally and reminisce about the good times and enjoy pleasant memories. But we need to be cognizant that many of our past memories are not useful. Some of them are emotionally damaging as well. Thinking of them is a waste of mental space, time and energy. We could have memories that are so bitter that recalling them can ruin our present and future. Let us stop entertaining negative or wasteful memories of pain, resentment, hurt, blame, anger or fear.

We have the power to control the working of our mind. We can exercise discretion over the thoughts we want to stop, the thoughts we want to relive and the thoughts we intend to carry into the future. Our past can have a far-reaching impact on our future. We cannot change what happened but we can choose what to carry with us going forward. We often do not realize the burden of the emotional baggage we are carrying, of our ignorance, pain, anger, attachments, expectations, wrong habits and people's opinions. Unpleasant past experiences are recorded in our minds in these ways: 'Why did this happen to me?', 'How can I ever be happy?', 'I am destined for a life of pain and suffering', 'I keep getting rejected ... No one needs me', etc. This means we have allowed our mind to stand in the way of our progress. If we do not let go of the past pain, we will create the same emotions each time the same or a similar stimulus comes up. This repeated reliving of pain will take a toll on our happiness and health.

It is certainly important that we acknowledge and take responsibility for our past—the rights, wrongs, mistakes, failures and pleasant and painful memories. Accountability helps us to reconcile with whatever has happened so that we do not live in denial. We do not let the negativity haunt us. We will also be able to learn from past situations to become wiser and stronger. Having said that, we do not need to live imprisoned in the past.

Leave the Past Behind

Our life experiences are recorded as memories. So we cannot just magically flush them out of our system and get rid of them. But what we can certainly do is overwrite past memories by creating new recordings that make us happy, peaceful, loving and forgiving. Moving into the future with less emotional baggage is a choice. In our own experience, we have already given considerable thought to expressions like 'forgive and forget', 'let go and move on' and 'seize the present moment'. But we have not applied these lines when a particular memory strikes. We have lost the present moment by brooding over something which ceases to exist.

We are aware of our innate, beautiful qualities. Now we are also aware and convinced that our impulsive reactions to unpleasant incidents are our own creation. No one else hurt, insulted, ignored, angered or troubled us. They just said or did what they felt was right. But it was our wrong thoughts and reactions that created the emotional wound. Today, we can heal the wound by creating right thoughts. We can stop blaming other people or situations involved in that incident. **How liberating it is to know that we do not have to wait for someone to apologize or some situation to change in order to release our pain. We created the hurt and we can heal the self.**

This realization changes our perception about the unpleasant past—the people involved, their words, their behaviour and the situation. As we create more and more thoughts of acceptance, as we think more lovingly, the mind starts storing new recordings and memories. New recordings of compassion, love and respect become reinforced. Consequently, the past wounds hurt less and less, and finally they all get completely healed. The memory is still present in our mind but it no longer hurts. This is similar to a physical wound we got in childhood, perhaps when we tripped and fell. Today, ten, twenty or forty years later, the scar might still be visible on our body but it does not hurt. We do not even think about it. We have forgotten about that wound because it is no longer obstructing our day-to-day activities. The same happens with emotional wounds. When it no longer hurts, it means forgiving, forgetting, letting go and moving on—have all already happened.

Affirmations can also be used to heal past hurt. When the inner conversation of the past repeats in the mind, we can consciously create new thoughts: 'I understand their sanskar

… The past is in the past … It's over … Full stop … I release … I let go … I forgive … I forget'.

Visualize the past impression leaving the subconscious mind. This can be done daily and repeatedly when the mind relives the past. Like we teach a child, we need to teach our mind to think right. Let us revisit the original thoughts of emotional baggage listed in the preceding section and change them to new, right thoughts:

- **Original thoughts**: *My parents love my sister more. They celebrated her fifth birthday and not mine.*
  New thoughts: *My parents have always loved my sister and me equally. They do their best for both of us, caring and supporting us unconditionally. I understand they had a reason for not celebrating my fifth birthday though they wanted to. I know they have nothing but pure intentions for me. I release the past … I understand my parents. I respect them. I love my family.*

- **Original thoughts**: *My friend hated that I was possessive about her. I should have been careful.*
  New thoughts: *I love my friend. She cares for me, I care for her. I accept her as she is. I am emotionally independent. When she spends time with others, I do not compare or compete with anyone. I value my friendship. I need nothing from her. I only radiate love, care and respect.*

- **Original thoughts**: *I will never forget the humiliation I faced during the university admission interview.*
  New thoughts: *I am a wise being. I achieve my goals. Sometimes, I make a mistake. I know I did my best. I*

understand that it was their perspective, it was their emotional state. I appreciate their feedback. I radiate compassion for their criticism. The past is in the past ... it is over. I take a determined decision to begin again.

When the emotional wounds from the past haunt us, what can we do to release them? Just five simple steps when followed systematically for a few days will free us from bitter memories:

Step 1: Identify the incident that you want to release.

Step 2: Examine your thoughts about that situation, including how you think about the people involved in it.

Step 3: Write down affirmations for it, similar to the examples shared above.

Step 4: Repeat them slowly every night before sleeping. Your pain will reduce gradually.

Step 5: Continue stating the affirmations until you experience that the incident no longer hurts you.

5

Taming Your Temper

H<small>E RETURNED AFTER A LONG DAY AT OFFICE. HIS WIFE</small> lovingly served dinner.

He groaned. 'Oh, not again. Why did you cook this?'

Banging the spoon on the table, he angrily stood up to leave. She instantly knew he was dumping his workplace frustration on her. He had done that several times.

She politely said, 'Please do not be angry. Please recall … I asked in the morning if you wanted this for dinner and you said yes. Anyway, let me quickly prepare something else.'

He replied, 'I do not want anything. You cannot cook well, speak well or dress well … you cannot do anything right.'

Wanting to calm him down, the wife offered a chair but he pushed it aside. She gave him a glass of water but he refused to drink. She pleaded with him to become calm but he yelled, 'I cannot!'

The doorbell rang. The husband opened the door. It was a courier delivery boy. That boy suddenly realized he was at the wrong address and apologized. The husband smiled and said, 'Never mind. You take care.' He closed the door.

The wife mumbled, 'You were angry with me for no fault of mine. But you were nice to him though he was at fault.'

He retorted, 'I cannot help it. It is you who always makes me angry. You bring out the worst in me.'

Most of us have been in similar situations. We have either been at the receiving end of someone's anger even when we did nothing wrong, or we have fumed at somebody even when they did nothing wrong.

What Pushes Your Anger Button?

As the most evolved beings on the planet, we enjoy taking control of every aspect of life. We even expect the world to submit to our idea of control. But when reality pans out differently, anger is the emotion we commonly create. We believe we are peaceful individuals and it is those irritating people or 'horrible situations' that make us angry.

Check if you believe in any of these statements about anger:

- *Other people and situations are the cause of my anger.*
- *Anger is a normal human reaction.*
- *Anger arises by itself.*
- *A little anger is harmless as it brings a rush of energy.*
- *Anger is necessary to get work done properly and in time.*
- *Anger is justified at times.*

We might cite different reasons to be angry: failure to meet our own expectations, other people not being our way, someone making mistakes, unfavorable situations or fatigue. If none of these reasons apply, we blame the stars, our horoscope or genes for our short temper. Nevertheless, we believe the cause for our anger is always external. But that is not true. **Anger is our choice and our internal creation. It is a result of our lack of self-control, lack of patience and lack of awareness to think the right way, in response to a situation.**

Anger begins in our mind at first as toxic or turbulent thoughts. When we do not control these thoughts, the turbulent energy creates impatience. As wrong thoughts accumulate further, they cause irritation. The next stage is of frustration. If we do not change our thoughts even at this point, our bitter feelings develop into anger. An extreme expression of our anger is called fury or rage. Notice how each subsequent stage becomes more uncomfortable.

Has Your Anger Been Useful?

- We spoil years of relationships by losing our temper **once**.
- We damage our reputation at the workplace by venting our frustration **once**.
- We lose a huge business deal by being rude to a customer **once**.
- We sustain physical injuries by getting involved in an incident of road rage **once**.

Just **one** episode of anger often makes us pay a heavy price, although our angry reaction is a result of irritation or frustration that has accumulated over a long time. Having been led to believe that anger is natural, necessary or obvious, most of us have created a habit of getting angry every now and then. This is why we often say things like:

- *The driver was late. I got angry. He promised to be punctual.*
- *I yelled at the plumber and he fixed the tap.*
- *The kids had messed up their room but cleaned it when I shouted at them.*

Perhaps anger did get us what we wanted externally—the driver, plumber, kids—everyone fell in line. But within the next few minutes, another issue came up and we continued using the same method, as it seemed to have once worked perfectly. We got results once again, so we believed anger works and is necessary. This is true to a large extent. People understand our disappointment, they obey us and get things done. But we do not realize that it is all happening at the cost of our happiness, health and relationships. Targeting someone with anger affects our relationship with them. When there are undercurrents in a relationship, the tasks we do will certainly not carry the right energy.

No matter how hard we try to justify anger, the fact remains that it is neither useful nor justified. Let us understand with an example: employees at an office are working comfortably, focused on their tasks. The CEO known for his aggressive and critical behavior, enters. Suddenly, the energy of the office changes. A heavy and uncomfortable silence sets in. He starts hovering over his staff at their desks. He stands behind an employee staring into the computer. That employee feels restless, scared and anxious. His fear radiates negativity into his mind, body, work and into the environment. As a result, the employee commits a mistake. The CEO quickly points at the error, embarrasses and warns the employee.

That employee feels terrible and cannot stop thinking of what happened. He just cannot focus on work. He feels powerless and intimidated. His ego gets hurt. He goes home early and shouts at his wife and children for trivial reasons, as if to prove to himself he is not weak. They feel scared. Their fear makes him feel slightly better. He tells himself, 'This is good. People fear me. I am powerful.' Effectively, the anger of the CEO had a cascading effect. The employee created anger, he was not efficient at work and his family started fearing him.

Now visualize the CEO to be of a peaceful and cheerful nature. Being a calming influence, he promotes a positive work culture. His energy empowers the employee perform to his potential. The employee goes home in a happy state of mind. His wife and children enjoy spending time with him. In this case, the calmness of the CEO had a cascading effect. The employee remained happy, he worked efficiently and his family bonded well with him.

Does Anger Impart a Sense of Empowerment?

Often when we remain silent and do not react, we are perceived as weak. But if we yell and speak in a loud tone, accompanied by aggressive body language, we are perceived as strong. Therefore, we hear people saying:

- *My silence will make everyone think I am a coward.*
- *If I keep quiet, they will take me for granted.*

We all know someone who speaks or behaves aggressively. They believe in arguing, venting, dominating or even punishing other people to feel powerful.

- *All I need to do is raise my voice, and my family immediately obeys me.*
- *When I get angry, no one dares to stand in front of me.*

There are people who resort to throwing things around, to express displeasure: a teacher throws a chalk, a parent throws household items and a boss throws files angrily. People start obeying them out of fear or helplessness, leading them to believe that anger gives them the power to control others.

Anger might give them **outer power**, which means power over people and situations but what they do not realize is that anger takes away their **inner power**. When we lack inner power, we try to make up for the deficiency by exerting power over other people. Wanting to control others becomes an addiction. The expectation of people doing things the way we want, the anxiety about getting someone to obey us and the disappointment if they disobey—each of these scenarios takes a toll on our mind. Our inner power reduces quickly.

When people obey us, we believe that we are powerful. But internally, our power keeps depleting for two reasons:

- **Firstly, our sense of power becomes dependent on other people. Dependency is depletive.**

- **Secondly, the people who are being controlled will feel humiliated, rejected and hurt. Their negative emotions are vibrations which reach us and deplete our energy.**

Other people cannot always be controlled. But because of our age, position in a relationship or status at work, we sometimes feel entitled to feel angry at others. Fear or helplessness might lead them to comply. But their hurt or painful feelings are equivalent to someone telling us day after day, 'I am unhappy and you are the reason for my unhappiness.' Every time a person holds us responsible for their pain, fear, sorrow and helplessness, we receive the highest form of negative energy from them. The moment they think of us or meet us, their energy gets disturbed. But we wrongly believe that people obeying us means they respect us. People who are afraid of us cannot respect us. When we are respected, pure and powerful energy comes to us from them. When we are feared, toxic and turbulent energy comes to us from them. **Fear and respect cannot coexist.**

Instead of controlling other people, we need to control our thoughts, words and behaviour. When we are in control of ourselves, we can be confident enough to tell the self, 'I am a powerful soul. Even if other people's behaviour or situations are not favourable, I remain calm. I remain stable.'

This is power—not over situations, not over people, but over the self.

Powerful souls understand that everyone is a soul on a journey. They realize that everyone carries sanskars that are different from their own. So, they accept that everyone's ways of thinking, speaking, behaving, living and working are bound to be different. Other people always being exactly how we want them to be is not normal. People always meeting our expectations is not normal. What is normal is for people to be different—not wrong, just different. What is normal is accepting our differences. What is normal is to live and work with dignity with different people while adjusting to their different sanskars.

An Investment that Guarantees Bitter Returns

If you believe anger is necessary, you tend to use it even in the most trivial circumstances. Even if you decide to be peaceful one day, you fail to sustain it. Have you considered for how long your anger could affect you? For starters, it is not limited to just the duration of your emotional outburst. Each time you get angry at someone, you actually make an energy investment, the return of which will keep coming to you until that person is emotionally healed. Let us understand the dynamics:

- **Your investment of anger depends on YOU**: The investment depends on the bitterness you create in terms of your intentions, words and behaviour. You are affected as soon as you create anger, since the creator of any emotion is the first receiver of its energy. How long you remain invested in anger depends on the extent and duration of your angry feelings.

- **The return of your anger depends on THEM**: The recipient of your anger might create hurt, resentment or hatred. Their painful vibrations radiate to you as they believe you are the cause of their pain. For how long you keep getting returns for the anger you invested depends on their emotional health. That person could take two minutes, two hours, two days, two weeks, two years, twenty years or a lifetime to heal. Until then, you receive their vibrations of pain, which subtly deplete your energy. The duration someone takes to heal does not depend on the intensity of your anger. It does not depend on their mistake either. It solely depends on their ability to release or let go of their disturbed feelings.

We make so many energy investments of anger, day after day, year after year, the returns of which keep coming. Sometimes, we cannot understand why we are unhappy, why we feel hollow or why we feel low. Now we know the reason—it is a return of our investment.

For your own protection, it is important to apologize to whoever you lose your temper at. Make it a personal principle to apologize to people for your anger, irrespective of their age, role or position. Your apology will help them to heal faster and you will stop receiving their vibrations of pain. For any reason if you are unable to apologize orally, send a message. Apologizing is not a sign of weakness, but rather a sign of strength. It reaffirms your understanding that anger is wrong, and so you can work towards eliminating that sanskar.

If you use compassion, that is also an investment whose returns will be pure wishes and blessings that come your way.

In this case, you may not even understand why you feel so light and happy—this again is a return of your investment.

Anger: A Matter of Choice

Do you lash out at elders at home? Do you yell at your boss? Do you shout at a three-month-old infant?

No, you do not. You remain patient and silent. At least, you refrain from saying anything to them, even if you disagree with them. This means you do not choose to be angry with people holding a certain position of power, seniority, role or responsibility.

Then, who do you get angry at? At those with who you believe it is all right to be angry or safe to be angry—perhaps your siblings, friends, spouse, children, peers or subordinates. This is good news because it brings back the ability to control anger. You are still at a stage where you are choosing to create anger. Note the word 'choosing'—you choose when and where to be angry, at whom and how much of anger to create. Take a moment to hammer this deep into your consciousness: **when you can choose patience with one person, you can choose it with anyone and everyone.**

Visualize two people in front of you, one of them angrily screaming, insulting and criticizing the other. The person getting scolded is simply looking down and not saying a word. What would your thoughts be? You might feel sorry for the person getting scolded. You pity his helplessness. Turns out, you are actually wrong to an extent. The one who creates anger suffers more than the one who receives it. Here is the reason:

- **The recipient of anger**: This person has a choice of either consuming the angry energy thrown at him or completely stop receiving it. For instance, if someone is known to be short-tempered, after a while, people stop getting affected when that person gets angry. They even become immune to the angry reactions. They might even laugh it off in their minds. They can become indifferent or stubborn. Essentially, they have an option whether or not to get affected. This is why we usually hear people even joke about an angry person: 'He will certainly shout today, but his anger no longer bothers me.'

- **The creator of anger**: The person creating anger is the first to experience the energy of anger. He cannot escape the toxic energy radiating to his mind, body, relationships and environment. We have already discussed the consequences of anger on emotional health. Besides, consequences on physical health can range from shivering, dryness of the mouth, headache, insomnia and high blood pressure to even cardiac arrest.

A study demonstrated that letting go of negative feelings that we may have for someone, relieves and reduces chronic backache. The soul is energy, and the body is matter. But the body also has an energy field, which is called the energy body. Today, there is technology to photograph the energy body, which reveals the region and extent of energy blockage. Before a person feels any discomfort in the body, the energy blockage can be detected. First, there is an energy blockage in the mind created due to turbulent emotions like anger, hurt, resentment, stress, fear, guilt and hatred. Next, it manifests as a blockage in the energy body. And much later, the energy blockage manifests into an illness in the physical body. We experience the symptoms only when it has reached the third stage, and so that is the stage which is treated by doctors. Doctors urge us to change our lifestyle so that the illness does not recur. We usually make changes to our dietary, exercise and sleep habits. What we fail to change are our emotional patterns.

Let us remember that our lifestyle also includes the way we think, speak, behave, work and live. Some of us have experienced energy healing, where a healing master cleanses the blockage in our energy body, or an emotional blockage in our subconscious, as a result of which we start feeling better physically also.

Be Assertive, Not Aggressive

Reacting angrily is not a big deal. Anyone can do it. When someone shouts at us, it is so easy to shout back louder or even raise our hand. But when someone criticizes, lies, behaves rudely or shies away from responsibilities, we actually need power if we want to respond peacefully. Everyone makes mistakes. Often, a mistake may just mean we do not do things the way the other person thinks is right. The ideal way of getting work done is to focus totally on the act, separating it from the person. Anger carries critical, negative and turbulent energy through thoughts and words. It is a subtle form of violence aimed at the other person who has not behaved the way we want them to. We use anger and want that person to feel bad, hurt, humiliated and, most importantly, accept his fault. Sometimes, we even bring up their past mistakes and unnecessarily complicate the matter.

We have reached a state where many people believe that only when we are loud or aggressive, our words are to be taken seriously, and not otherwise. We need to break this belief. We can do it only when we shift from anger to assertiveness. Being assertive enables us to focus on the task and the next steps to take. Peace and dignity reflect in our character. We do not target the people who make mistakes, so we keep our respect for them intact. When we treat someone respectfully, we will not have to get them to work for us. They will want to work for us because of the pure energy we radiate. This implies we do not find the need to raise our voice to be heard, understood or obeyed. Let us create a new belief system and tell ourselves: **'Anger is damaging, assertiveness is the way to get work done.'** Let us experiment with this and see the results.

Getting a Handle on Anger

Today there are places where heavy punching bags are hung for people to release their anger. Photos of the person they are angry at are sometimes stuck on these bags before the punches are delivered.

Recall the era of writing letters to people, when we did not have phones or instant messaging. In those times if we were angry about a person or situation, we would of course write a strong letter spilling all our anger into it. But by the time we purchased an envelope, wrote the message and stuck the postage stamp, sometimes hours or days would have passed. By then, our anger would have been doused significantly, and so we would decide not to post the letter. The time gap made sure that the situation did not escalate.

In the present times we use phones and emails to text or talk about every detail of our lives as it happens. So the moment we create an angry thought, we vent to someone. At times, that person endorses our reaction, thereby fuelling our anger. This unnecessary communication escalates the situation. This is why elders advise us to count from one to ten, take a few deep breaths or drink water as soon as we start feeling angry—so that we introduce a time gap between the stimulus and our response.

We are often told, 'Suppressing anger will hurt you a lot more than expressing it.' Indeed, supressing any negative emotion—not just anger—is toxic for both mind and body. But venting anger is equally damaging.

Think about this: what happens when we do not let anger out? Each time we create anger, we are the first to experience its negative energy. Subsequently, we receive negative energy from the person who is the target of our anger. Besides, each time we vent, we intensify our sanskar of anger. For these reasons, we need to learn to not create anger, and even if we create it, it is important to immediately change our thoughts and heal. Let us understand this with an example: suppose someone makes a mistake and you get angry, there are a few simple steps to defuse your anger.

Step 1: Do not express your anger although internally you may be angry.

Step 2: You might create these types of thoughts:

- *Why did he do this?*
- *How could he not even inform me?*
- *I should not have trusted him.*
- *He always makes this mistake.*

If you express your anger with words, the other person might react and defend himself, which will make you angrier. But now you choose not to say anything to him.

Step 3: It might be tempting to instantly send that person a message or email. It is crucial that you resist that urge.

Step 4: Instead of writing to someone else, write a message to yourself to help change your thoughts. This ensures you do not suppress anger but instead address it. For instance, you can write, 'He should have not done it without discussing it with me. But he must have had a reason. I will ask him respectfully. I am ready to understand his perspective.'

Step 5: Notice two things that happen when the mind obeys your instruction: your willpower increases and your anger starts diluting. Today you stopped at four thoughts. The next time you might create only three thoughts. So as you resolve the anger outside, gradually and with understanding, knowledge and soul power, anger gets eliminated internally in your thoughts as well.

Step 6: Using only positive words, speak or write to that person who has made a mistake. Appreciate that person for his strengths. And then suggest a way to rectify his mistake. Without accusing or criticizing, share your expectations about his ways of working or behaving.

When you put your ego aside and then write or speak, you actually empower the other person also to put aside ego and listen. This prevents ego clashes or arguments and encourages a mutually respectful dialogue.

Six Steps to Evade the Anger Trap

The sanskar of anger can be so deep that we barely realize how it displaces peace completely. Peace is not just the absence of anger but our very state of being, which translates into pure thoughts, kind words and courteous behaviour. Peace is the antidote to anger. Mastering these six steps can erase the angry habit and restore peace.

Step 1: Observe your state of mind the moment there is a slight disturbance, like traces of impatience, irritation or edginess. This awareness will help you take steps to arrest the emotion well before it turns into full-blown anger. Apart from watching your thoughts when you feel unpleasant, check your thoughts after every hour or two.

Step 2: Take complete responsibility for your disturbing thoughts and feelings. Your mind will be tempted to hold external factors responsible. Counsel the mind by saying, 'I am responsible for how I think and feel. My irritation is my creation. I overcome it.' Your mind takes time to agree, especially when the other person is clearly wrong or when a situation is clearly unfavourable. Patiently and lovingly counsel it as many times as needed to bring back responsibility to the self. Self-counselling gradually changes your thoughts and then your responses to situations will change, helping you gradually overcome anger.

Step 3: Identify the reason for the inner turbulence. Anger is mostly an outcome of attachment towards a person, object, place, position or task. For instance, if someone makes a mistake, your anger is not about their mistake. It is most likely due to your attachment to that task or that person. You believe their mistake will cost you dearly, or because you care so much for that person, you cannot tolerate them making mistakes. At this moment remind yourself, 'I am a trustee. I take care of everything but nothing belongs to me. I use calmness and patience in my roles and responsibilities.'

Step 4: Accept the circumstance, understanding that people and situations are not in your control. Moreover, it has already happened. The past has passed. There is no point wasting time or energy creating anger by accusing, shouting, blaming or reprimanding. Focus on the two-stepped response: focus on your state of mind first and then on the solution.

Step 5: Remind yourself, 'I am a peaceful being. Peace comes naturally in response to whatever happens. No matter what has happened, I will respond my way—the right way—with patience, assertiveness and compassion. My peaceful mind enables me to resolve the issue.' You can reaffirm these thoughts once every morning, once at night before sleep and any number of times during the day. This programmes your mind to respond the right way.

Step 6: As anger subsides, your peace builds up. In this peaceful state, you are likely to find a quick and accurate solution to the current issue. Inner success in terms of stability, comfort and inner power will influence outer success. Now make corrections or discipline people assertively.

Create No-anger Zones

Until a few years ago, people were allowed to smoke cigarettes even in public spaces. Later, several countries identified specific spaces where smoking was prohibited. This led to the creation of no-smoking zones in the interest of non-smokers. Can we not apply the same rule for anger, knowing well that it is harmful for us and for the people around us? We can each make it a personal law that our home and workplace will be no-anger zones. Creative posters or signs can be put up to convey 'This is a No-anger Zone' at strategic spots at your home, office, shop, hospital, school and college. This will be a huge step in the direction of eradicating anger and reducing disrespect, fear, anxiety and hurt around you.

We already have a clearly defined 'No-anger Zone' in our mind when we interact with certain people. As discussed earlier, we do not get angry with those who are in a position of power in terms of age, role, authority or designation. Why not expand its boundaries to let everybody inside? There are simple steps that can yield great results in ending anger.

Step 1: Identify two family members and two colleagues with whom you often lose your temper. The moment you feel an urge to snap at them, pause.

Step 2: Do not allow anger to come into your words or behaviour. Restrict it at the level of thoughts.

Step 3: Remind yourself lovingly, 'I am a powerful being, living in a no-anger zone. I understand they have a reason for what they did. I use patience and acceptance. It is my protection and empowerment.'

Step 4: Notice your anger subsiding and eventually ceasing. Now talk to the person with patience and acceptance. Give them the necessary correction, advice, opinion, instruction or a warning, as the case may be. Even if you are having to take a disciplinary action, do it assertively but not angrily.

Step 5. Every week, move more and more people into the no-anger zone.

Establishing no-anger zones as a personal discipline creates a space in our mind and our surroundings for peaceful and open communication. It lets us conserve physical and emotional energy and thereby boost inner power. Even if things go wrong, we will have the resources—mind power and people power—to come together to resolve the issue.

6

Stress No More

HAVING SETTLED COMFORTABLY ON THE COUCH, YOU are watching a thriller movie. Its riveting storyline and brilliant performances have you hooked. Just when a plot twist unfolds, there is a commercial break. You obviously know that commercial breaks are inevitable, but you lose your calm since the action you were waiting to enjoy, has been slowed down. The timing is wrong and the interruption is long. So while waiting for the movie to resume, you criticize and blame the TV channel for ruining the viewing experience.

In a way, emotional stress works similar to this—actually, we let it work this way. We want our life to flow smoothly without interruptions. But just as we begin to enjoy a particular scene, there comes an interruption which slows things down. We feel annoyed. We feel stressed. And we blame that interruption for our stress. We even let the stress remain until the scene resumes normally.

Not all of us are familiar with the definition of emotional stress, but most of us have experienced it to a point where it can be called a global epidemic. This has led us to believe that a little stress is natural and obvious. We often talk about 'managing' or 'coping' with stress, instead of 'eliminating' it altogether, as though it is an inevitable reality of life. **In its basic form, emotional stress is a pain which occurs to tell us there is something we need to change internally in our mind. There is either something that we want and are not getting, or there is something we do not want but have in our life—we create emotional pain in either of these cases.** This pain hampers our very nature of being happy, peaceful and healthy individuals. The disturbed state of mind in turn makes our daily tasks harder to handle when stress trickles into every aspect of life—personal wellbeing, relationships and career.

The Stressors in Your Life

What is the cause of stress in your life? Perhaps you have so many answers to this that you cannot really pinpoint one factor and say, 'This is it'. For instance, cooking is enjoyable for someone. It stresses out someone else. Someone thrives under pressure. Someone else feels stressed even at the thought of pressure. One person enjoys parenting and another finds it stressful. Somebody does not mind working fifteen hours a day while somebody else feels stressed about just five hours of work. Essentially, what one person finds easy can be stressful for another. But in general, we hold various situations responsible: deadlines, exams, routines, performance pressure, challenges, relationships, conflicts, disagreements, expectations, peer pressure, competition, goals, past experiences, failures, meetings, work, finances, illness, separation, death, change … one can keep adding to this list.

The Culprit Is Closer than You Think

Stressors are what we believe are the cause of our stress, and stress is what we believe is our natural response to them. But is that true? How many times do we find ourselves and people around us saying:

- *I have an exam, obviously I will feel stressed.*
- *My child does not study well, obviously I am stressed.*
- *Thinking of my low bank balance stresses me out.*

It is easy to blame external factors for our stress as it means we do not have to take personal responsibility. We mostly wait for situations to get sorted—for health to improve, for the boss to be kinder, for our spouse to be more understanding, for exams to be easier to crack, for children to behave better, for a business to flourish—so that our stress would come down. Even if we take action to change circumstances, we tend to do it with a disturbed state of mind, creating negative emotions like worry, anxiety, fear, insecurity, aggression, irritation or anger.

Life brings unexpected events before us. We can control only a small fraction of them. Yet, we set expectations of how scenes should unfold and get emotionally attached to our expectations, believing that is what is right for us. Therefore, each time there is a change—although we know change is inevitable—we have a fight or flight response. We hesitate to come out of our comfort zone. We try to reject or escape it. When our apprehensive thoughts accumulate in the mind, our inner power reduces. We experience an inner discomfort, an inner weakness, an inner pain, and this pain is stress.

Recall the situation of the world when the coronavirus pandemic set in. It imposed huge changes in several aspects of our lifestyle. Our thoughts had the negative energies of fear, apprehension and panic—not just for a few days but for several months. As a result, millions across the globe created stress. On the other hand, a few people who accepted the changes and adapted to them, experienced little to no stress. Embracing the changes enabled these people to silence the mind and focus on solutions. They utilized the lockdown for self-care, having understood the importance of good health for both the mind and body. They practised meditation and yoga, engaged in serving others and spent time with their families. Such individuals came out empowered, at a time when others felt overwhelmed.

Consider another example: Until five years ago, most people looked forward to the weekend. They felt workplaces were stressful. Today, they have started feeling that family life is stressful. The truth is: neither is the workplace stressful nor the family. Neither do projects create stress nor children. It is our uncomfortable thoughts day after day, year after year, that deplete our energy.

Thus, stress is not a result of what happens in our life. Stress is a result of our incorrect response to situations. As we know, our response is formed by the beliefs we hold and thereby the thoughts we create.

- Stress is not caused by situations; it is caused by the way we think in every situation.
- Stress is not caused by people; it is caused by the way we think and feel about them.
- Stress is not caused by obstacles, failures or setbacks in life; it is caused by the way we perceive our efforts and results.

It is easy to point the finger of blame for our stress in other directions. The good news is that we have decided to take personal responsibility for how we think and feel in every situation. We are the creators of our stress and we are perfectly capable of becoming stress-free. If the world was the cause of our stress, then we can never be stress-free because the world will not function the way we want it to. But our mind can get rid of stress completely, and this awareness is power. This is liberation. This shreds away the long list of causes of our stress and puts us on track to get rid of stress completely. The first secret to eliminate stress is to know that being stress-free is an easily achievable goal. The second secret is to know that one person can do it: the self.

All we need is to pay attention to our thoughts and feelings through self-care. When we do this, our spiritual, emotional, mental, physical, social and professional health will heal in ways which we had never imagined.

How Effective Are De-Stressors?

Many young children are fascinated by fire. Out of natural curiosity, some of them touch the flame of a lit candle, a lighter or a matchstick. The incredibly painful burn on their finger teaches them a lesson. They receive the message to be careful and not play with fire again. Similarly, when we experience stress, we need to learn the lesson: to change our response. But often, we find ourselves resorting to watching TV, shopping, partying, holiday, smoking or consuming alcohol and other such distractions when stressed. Do any of these thoughts sound familiar?

- *Music is my biggest de-stressor.*
- *Nothing like a vacation to break free from stress.*
- *Let us watch a movie to relieve this stress.*
- *A spa treatment is so soothing, it removes my stress.*
- *Lighting up a cigarette makes me forget my stress.*

Unfortunately, none of them are de-stressors. They are merely temporary deviators or distractors from the sensation of pain. These distractions can only help us take a break, change the environment or relax the body. But none of them can remove stress. Stress is emotional pain in the mind, and the mind is our child within. Leaving a child to cry for long is never a good idea. Instead, if we take five minutes to address the problem and counsel the mind with the right thoughts, the child that is our mind will stop crying.

Suppose a person has a tooth decay causing him pain. It requires dental treatment. However, he thinks, 'This novel is supposedly a bestseller. Let me read it. I will feel better.' His thoughts thus shift from pain towards a different pattern of pleasure based on the storyline. The pain is subdued or masked temporarily. Sure enough, he does feel the ache returning, when he puts the book down. The question is: What happens if he keeps distracting his mind from pain for hours or for days? The problem will no longer remain just a tooth decay. The infection will spread and lead to complications. The same happens with untreated stress—or any other negative emotion, for that matter. The longer we keep distracting our mind from stress, the more it intensifies.

Today, there are umpteen distractions. So, we find it easier to divert our mind towards them than to heal emotional pain. We are not even aware that we are distracting our disturbed mind; we have made the distractions a normal part of our life. When was the last time you sat just with yourself, doing nothing— without even reaching for the phone, the TV remote or a book? Gone are the times when we would ease into being alone and relish solitude. Some of us feel uncomfortable being alone with ourselves. Now we feel lonely when on our own even for an hour or two. In fact, some of us feel lonely even in the company of people. This can be a symptom of deeper issues like anxiety, stress or depression.

Make it a practice to sit doing nothing for a few minutes every day, away from all distractions and follow these simple steps to see how you can diagnose your thoughts and begin healing your mind.

Step 1: Begin with five minutes of 'me time' and gradually increase the duration. You will become aware of what is troubling your mind.

Step 2: Write those thoughts down to understand them better. Let your ideas flow freely. Writing them helps you identify what is causing negative or wasteful thoughts. Those are the thoughts which need healing and can otherwise lead to stress.

Step 3: Be a friend to yourself and start writing the answer to your thoughts, just like you would reply to the messages of your friend. Write as though you are helping them to resolve their issues and pulling them out of their pain.

Step 5: Observe how the activity of writing out the answers will help you think differently and, most importantly, with a detached outlook. Your mind may not be healed right away but you will start looking at the problem with a new perspective.

Step 6: Sit with your mind again the next day and the next … until you arrive at a solution.

Step 7: Implement the solution on yourself.

It is possible that the solution is not something that has to be implemented outside. Situations like death have no solution but the mind needs to be healed from the pain of loss. Soon you will master the art of healing yourself. Your stability will influence and empower others. This practice of 'Me-time' will equip you over a period to reach a stage where you will not even create pain in the first place, as your mind would have learnt the right way of thinking.

Recognize the Warning Signs

Contrary to popular belief, stress is not caused because of more responsibilities or working for fifteen hours a day. One can complete a thousand tasks each day while remaining calm, happy and easy with absolutely no trace of stress. Stress has nothing to do with the 'doing'. It is all about the state of 'being'. It is all about how we think and feel in every instance. So, it is important to examine our mind and recognize any symptoms of stress.

Whenever there is discomfort in your mind, pause and check:

- Were your thoughts negative or wasteful?
- Did you feel overwhelmed or helpless?
- Were your words and behaviour rude, critical or aggressive?

Here are a few pointed questions to drill down and introspect further:

- Were you upset about yourself or someone else?
- Were you scared, irritated, angry or frustrated about a situation?

- Was your mind preoccupied with questions like why, what, what if, but then …?
- Were you dwelling on the past or worrying about the future?
- Were you doing any task unwillingly?
- Were you hurrying yourself or other people?

Even if you cannot diagnose at the level of thoughts and feelings, you can easily check how you felt physically:

- How were your bodily sensations?
- Did you experience shortness of breath, faster heartbeat, perspiration, trembling hands, dryness in the mouth, heaviness in the head and so on?

If your answer is a 'yes' to any of these questions, it becomes your responsibility to take immediate action to change your thoughts. You owe it to your mind. Otherwise, wrong thinking patterns created over a period of time will create stress.

The Science of Stress

Even twenty-five to thirty years ago, people faced several challenges. Yet no one said, 'I feel stressed.' Stress was just a term explained in Physics textbooks and classrooms. It was not a part of conversations to refer to the state of mind. Today, most of us like to say, 'I am stressed.' We feel it conveys that we are busy, we are going the extra mile and we are more successful. In other words, sometimes we wield the word 'stress' as a status symbol. Unfortunately, society today has too many people competing to see who is more stressed.

The word 'stress' is often used interchangeably with 'pressure'. For example, a target or deadline at office is a pressure on us but we wrongly term it as 'work stress'. An exam is a pressure on us but we wrongly call it 'exam stress'.

The formula for stress is:

Stress = Pressure / Resilience
[Stress is equal to Pressure divided by Resilience]

where

- Numerator: Pressure = External situations like pandemics, exams, targets, health, goals, money, job loss, time, traffic, relationships, weather and so on.

   Pressure refers to the situations coming to us. Pressure is an external factor that is not always under our control. Today, pressures have increased. There are more changes in the education system, work culture, expectations in relationships, lifestyle, social conditioning and so on.
- Denominator: Resilience = Our inner strength, including our consciousness, perspective, thoughts, feelings, words, actions, qualities, values and principles.

> Resilience is our inner power to face pressure. We are the creators of our resilience, and it is always under our control. Under any situation, 10 per cent depends upon the pressure and 90 per cent depends upon our resilience.
>
> **Therefore, stress is equal to our situations divided by our inner strength.**

Stress is not caused because of increased pressures. It is caused by reduced resilience. Our lifestyle has also been feeding stress. Many of us are only too familiar with these habits that are reducing resilience: sleep deprivation, junk food consumption, plugging into technology constantly, too much screen time, toxic content consumption and emotional adjustment issues. In the process, we have ignored powerful practices like spiritual study and meditation.

Your Ability to Bounce Back

Consider the cycle of seasons. If it is summer today, in a few months it will be monsoon. We will not just sit at home saying 'It is raining'. We say, 'Never mind if it rains. I am ready with my raincoat and umbrella.' We protect ourselves and do not blame the weather. Likewise, we need to learn the mechanism of protecting our emotional state from adversities by becoming resilient.

Pressures certainly do not seem to be abating; they are only going to increase. Let us not become so focused on controlling the pressures that we do not seem to have the time to enhance our resilience. Resilience is like a muscle that we can develop and strengthen, rather than a quality we are born with. Suppose an employee is given a deadline of twenty-four hours to complete his project report. It is a target or pressure. It is important to set targets because otherwise he might take four days to finish it. But the minute he is told, 'Complete this by tomorrow evening', he starts panicking. Suppose he starts creating these thoughts:

- *This is scary. How will I finish the report by tomorrow evening?*
- *If I do not complete this task in time, how will my future in this company look?*
- *My report was not up to the mark last time. I better do a good job now.*

This means he is working on the task with a stressed mind. Suppose his teammate is also asked to prepare a report independently within the same deadline and she thinks:

- *I am focused. I can do anything I decide to do.*
- *I will certainly complete this easily by tomorrow evening.*
- *This will be my best presentation till date.*

This means she starts off with faith and determination.

Both will eventually complete the report, which means both will reach the destination, but their journeys will be different. One will reach there creating stress because of negative thoughts. The other will reach with stability because of powerful thoughts.

Seven Life Skills to Beat Stress

We are supposed to build immunity by following a good diet and exercising every single day. It is never going to be enough if we start eating healthy and exercise on the day that we fall ill. Resilience works the same way. We need to build it systematically, daily—not once a week and not only when time permits. It cannot be created overnight by sitting in meditation or creating affirmations on the day an adversity strikes.

Here are seven skills that increase your resilience every day. They create an inner shift in your ways of being, ways of thinking and ways of living.

Skill 1: Write Your Story, Not Theirs

We are the scriptwriters, directors and actors of our movie of life. But throughout the day, when we watch or interact with others, we keep writing mental scripts of how they are, how they should be and what they should do. In the process we forget to sort, fix or perfect our own role. Thinking of someone else is an unnecessary pressure we put on ourselves. Our co-actors are responsible for their roles. They write their own scripts and follow them.

Focus on perfecting your own performance. Do not think about other people. Let your style and your personality of peace, love and kindness reflect in every scene of your life. Create what you enjoy watching. Even if other actors don't perform right, your performance can give them a cue to correct themselves.

Remind yourself: 'In every scene I focus on my role, my script. I bring out my style of peace and power with right thoughts, pure words and perfect behaviour.'

Skill 2: Make Acceptance Natural

All of us hold a desire that the world should bend to our wants. And when it does not, we start whining or questioning the circumstance. We even dislike ourselves, our home, family, friends or career in such moments. It means we do not go with the flow. We try to block or push away the reality in our thoughts and feelings. Most of our stress comes from this inner struggle to wrestle with the natural flow. Our stiff resistance becomes a barrier to peace. Besides, the act of resisting depletes inner power and creates stress.

Do not ask why, where, when or how difficult experiences inevitably occur. Shift from asking 'What is this?' to accepting as 'This is it'. When you surrender to the reality instead of resisting it, you conserve energy. This conserved energy can then be used to focus on solutions and new possibilities. Start with acceptance of people and situations and then influence them or empower them to change. Be open to newness and changes.

Remind yourself: 'I accept whatever is happening. People and situations will be their way. I remain calm and influence them to change.'

Skill 3: Choose Your Words Wisely

Words are the most powerful tools at our disposal, but they are often underrated. Many of us are in the habit of speaking far more than is necessary. Whether it is to ask, inform, explain, advise, convince or impress, we tend to overthink and hence over-speak. This urge to speak does not leave the margin to choose our words carefully, add value or speak pleasantly. It becomes difficult for us to connect with our inner peace. Excessive talking depletes our energy and eventually increases stress.

Practise speaking less throughout your day. After a few weeks, begin to speak more softly. Observe your vocabulary and eliminate low-energy or negative words. Gradually, your words will raise your vibrations, the vibrations of situations and of the people around you. You will be more at ease with yourself.

Remind yourself: 'I speak less, speak softly and speak sweetly. I create peace by choosing words that energize and empower.'

Skill 4: Flip Negative Labels

All through our life, people bombard us with labels for who we are—or are not—based on our achievements, appearance, background, personality or possessions. Negative labels are risky because we come to believe them and accept those labels as our reality. When we repeat them over and over in our thoughts, our mind and body respond and start living by that label. This causes us to feel bad or dislike ourselves. Nothing is more stressful than self-hate.

Review the labels you describe yourself with. Replace every single negative label with a pure, powerful, positive label. If you have called yourself a failure, write down the things you have succeeded in. Make them your vocabulary, repeat them consistently for a few days until they stick and get reinforced as your truth. Feeling good about yourself is a huge step in experiencing peace.

Remind yourself: 'I label myself with only and only positive words. I'm aware that my labels manifest my destiny.'

Skill 5: Listen to the Tutor Within

We take dozens of decisions every single day, and at times struggle to discern rights and wrongs. The doubt and deliberation can become stressful. Fortunately, we have all the answers we seek within us. Our innate wisdom (inner voice, intellect, intuition or gut feeling) in the subconscious mind is always active and guides us correctly. We have all experienced our intuition at work. We say, 'I wish I had listened to my instincts' or 'Something tells me this is not good for me.' All we need is to listen to it. Otherwise, our responses will be driven by the stored patterns of our old sanskars.

Spend a few minutes with yourself in silence every day. Introspect on the consequences of your actions before choosing your karma. That is when you will hear the intuition.

Do not doubt that inner voice. And do not fear any challenges that might come up after you execute intuitive decisions. **Remember that your intuition always knows what is right for you.**

Remind yourself: 'I am intuitive. Each time I need to take a decision, I calm my mind and surrender to the wisdom within, and it always gives me the right answer.'

Skill 6: Make Trusteeship a Lifestyle

We are bestowed with so much in life—body, relationships, achievements, material possessions and natural resources. We are supposed to take care of them and use them as trustees. But somehow, we assume ownership of everything that we have and become emotionally attached to them. Where there is attachment, there will be fear of losing. And where there is fear, there will be stress. Despite knowing that we will eventually lose all that we possess, we still cling on to them and hope to never part with anything.

Practise a new consciousness—instead of ownership, be a trustee. Change how you relate to whatever you feel attached to. A trustee knows that he is entrusted to manage someone else's assets. So as a trustee, you can take better care because it would be caring without fear, possessiveness or control. This will keep your mind at ease and relaxed.

Remind yourself: 'I value and care for everything I have. I am not attached to or dependent on anything. I am fearless. I am a trustee.'

Skill 7: Transcend Illusions about Yourself

Self-awareness is a precursor to emotional stamina. Unfortunately, many of us do not know our reality as souls even after having lived for thirty, fifty or seventy years. Even if we know, we keep identifying with the body and the labels of roles, positions and achievements. We first stress about gaining all of them and then stress about holding onto them. After all, how we perceive ourselves influences how we see the world around us. Regaining the awareness of the self puts a lid on our illusions. Stabilizing the truth of the self being a peaceful soul helps us to easily recognize emotions like fear, anxiety or pain, which can otherwise leave us stressed.

You are a soul who is an embodiment of peace and power. Hold on to this truth so tightly that the awareness does not slip away while you keep acquiring possessions or positions in life. Roles, positions and achievements certainly deserve your time and attention but do not let them steer you away from your real identity.

Remind yourself: 'I am a soul. I am peace. I am love. I am power. I radiate peace and happiness.'

Stress triggers several other disturbing emotions that in turn lead to unpleasant consequences. Therefore, do not settle for 'managing' or 'reducing' stress. A little inner work is all it takes to eliminate it completely. **Remember that shifting to a stress-free life is easily achievable because it depends only on one person: yourself.**

7

Ego and Its Tricks

SUPPOSE YOUR LIVING ROOM WINDOW OVERLOOKS THE sea. Your favourite part of your morning routine is to throw the windows wide open, stand by the windowpane sipping tea and take in the scenic view of the world outside—the calm sea, the breeze, the sunrise, the horizon, the boats, the birds, the people, the sounds ... you do not want to trade that serenity for anything. One day, your family places a wide cupboard right against that window, in a way that the window cannot be opened beyond two inches. How does the outside view appear now? What should have been a normal view is obstructed. The narrow opening robs you of the big picture. You are blinded to all the beauty that is right in front of you. You certainly do not like what you see. You feel disappointed, angry and hurt. You immediately get the cupboard removed, and there it is—the beautiful landscape becomes visible again.

This three-part scenario is comparable to what happens to us when we see the world—first when we are egoless, next when ego blocks our mind and finally when ego is pushed away. Unfortunately, nearly the whole of mankind is trapped by their egos today. This is the reason we do not like what we are seeing in our life. Much like the cupboard that obstructed the view, ego stands as a barrier between us and the truth, between us and the purity in other people, between us and the beauty in this world. Ego is the reason we are experiencing only a little peace, a little love, a little happiness and a little power. We do not experience these feelings in a lasting, natural way since ego stops us from seeing who we truly are and who everyone else truly is. The moment we get rid of ego, our world becomes beautiful, both on the inside and outside.

The 'Ego Problem'

'Ego' is an old, popular word we are all familiar with. We often refer to it in our conversations, yet we do not seem to know what it means. There are so many connotations attached to this word across society that it can be very confusing to get a grasp of what it means, what it looks like, what it does to us and what we must do with it.

Here are a few examples of how ego is understood and used in conversations:

- *Everyone in their family is egoistic.*
- *His ego got hurt.*
- *She pampers my ego and I enjoy it.*
- *Please rise above your ego.*
- *A little ego is necessary.*

To be fair, most people consider ego to be a negative trait, something they need to get away from. You may recall that ego makes it to the list of the top five vices of a human soul: lust, anger, greed, attachment and ego. But there is a small percentage who believe that ego is important or even inevitable. So, let us first understand what ego means. We shall start with an elementary question.

How would you answer this: 'Who am I?'

Perhaps the most frequently used word in our vocabulary is 'I'. What does this 'I' refer to when we talk about who we are? Primarily, we link our identity with all the things that we acquire or possess in life—our name, academic achievements, qualification, job title, roles, relationships, responsibilities and so on. Or we use it to refer to our gender, family, nationality, race or religion. Typically, our answers hover around identities similar to these examples:

- *I am Rohit/Riya/Payal/Vikas.*
- *I am a Hindu/Muslim/Christian/Sikh.*
- *I am an Indian/American/Malaysian/Korean.*
- *I am a Gujarati/Punjabi/Malayali.*
- *I am a student/doctor/swimmer/CEO/pensioner.*
- *I am a father/husband/daughter/wife/client.*
- *I am tall/fat/attractive.*

Notice that each of the above is just a label—a label applied on us either by ourselves or by other people. We know who we are through these labels—at least, that is what we think. But it turns out, that is not our reality. And that is the problem with ego. It gives us a wrong sense of our identity.

You may ask: 'What is wrong with that? Everyone defines themselves through these labels.'

Yes, everyone sees themselves as this, that or the other label. It seems a normal thing to do. But let us remember that several aspects that are untrue and wrong, have been passed off as normal in the world today.

Are Your Acquired Labels Insignificant?

Our acquired labels are by no means insignificant. Let us be clear that everything we acquire along the journey of life is valuable. The importance of our position, role, achievements and possessions are never to be undermined. Despite them being transient or temporary, they certainly keep us going and make our life interesting.

- We have acquired this body. We need to take care of it and keep it healthy.
- We have acquired relationships. We need to love and care for people unconditionally.
- We have acquired roles and responsibilities. We need to discharge them to the best of our abilities.
- We have acquired positions. We need to keep improving and growing further.

Acquiring all that we can is important. The only change needed is in our consciousness of what constitutes our identity. Let us stop identifying ourselves through acquisitions. This brings us to another question: How do we treat the acquired labels? Isn't it a fact that we are a mother, a friend, a professional or an Indian? Everything is a fact, except for the consciousness: 'I AM so and so'. Let us understand this with examples:

Name: I am Mr Vijay/Ms Preeti.
It is MY name; it is not I.

Profession: I am a carpenter/teacher.
It is MY profession; it is not I.

Relationship: I am a friend/spouse.
It is MY relationship; it is not I.

Nationality: I am an Indian.
It is MY nationality; it is not I.

Religion: I am a Hindu/Christian.
It is MY religion; it is not I.

We can now see how easily we confuse 'I' with 'MY'.

Are You What You See in the Mirror?

One of the most dangerous beliefs we have is that we are the image we see in the mirror. Looking at our body, we say:

- I have grown fat.
- I am looking perfect.
- I should have been taller.

We use the word 'I' for what we see in the mirror. We also say:

- *My stomach is hurting.*
- *My face is swollen.*
- *My body is aching today.*

Let us pause and check:
Is it: 'I AM the face', 'I AM the hands', 'I AM the body'?
Or is it: 'MY face', 'MY hands' 'MY body'?

Visualize yourself and your body. Do you feel you are the mouth, the feet and the eyes? Or do you feel you are the one who controls them? We have been using the words 'my' and 'I' interchangeably without checking if it was right or wrong. Let us examine it now. A moment of self-reflection reveals the answer that we already know. Someone is taking ownership, calling the body 'mine'. Who is it that is saying 'This is my body'?

How Ego Conceals Our Identity

When you refer to your vehicle, you say 'This is my car.'

What if you referred to your car as 'I' instead of 'my'? It would be both strange and incorrect.

We make the same mistake with our body. The body is a vehicle which we use at every moment of our life. But instead of referring to it as 'my body', we called it 'I'.

If we reflect on our life, we can see that the first entity we acquire is the body. Then we get parents and thereby comes the identity of being their child. That is followed by other relationships—we are someone's grandchild, sibling, cousin and so on. Later, we are given a name, the label which will be used to address us for the rest of our life. Once we start going to school, we acquire the labels of being a student and a friend to someone. As time goes by, our roles and responsibilities change. We keep acquiring new labels based on our qualification, designation, status, relationships, and so on. This can continue till the last day of our life. But we ignorantly make every label our identity and believe, 'This is who I am'.

So everything we are supposed to refer to as 'my', we wrongly refer to as 'I', thus creating a wrong image of the 'I'. Believing ourselves to be that image, over a period of time, we get attached to it. Attachment means that our state of mind becomes dependent on that image. As we saw earlier, emotional dependency means our feelings and emotions depend completely on how our body appears, how healthy the body is, how people behave with us, how professionally successful we are and what we achieve, acquire or possess. Do you think you are emotionally attached to your car? You might believe that you are not. If someone scratches your car, do you feel the pain? If someone bumps into your car, do you lose your patience and peace? If yes, you are emotionally dependent on the car, which means you are emotionally attached to it. You can spend some time to make a list of objects, people, places or situations on which you are emotionally dependent.

Emotional Dependency = Emotional Attachment

We develop emotional attachments with our body, relationships, roles, objects and even our ideas and opinions. And that is what creates ego. There are various ways in which ego is understood: as self-perception, self-centredness, superiority, arrogance, false pride, false identity.

Here is a definition of ego that sums up all the above ideas. You are encouraged to spend a little time and reflect on it:

Ego is attachment to a wrong image of myself.

Consider a man who has a physical body to use for eighty years. During his lifetime, he also acquires various relationships, roles, wealth, property and so on. First, he is a son, a grandson, a sibling, a friend, a cousin and so on. Years later, he becomes a father, and subsequently, a grandfather. He is bound to meet and lose people too. In his professional endeavours, his roles and designations keep changing every few years. He may start as a trainee engineer and move up the ranks to become the chairman of his organization. Someday, he retires but the attachment to his position can be so deep that he holds on to it as his identity. He even includes 'ex-' or 'retd.' as a prefix to his erstwhile designation on his nameplate. When he dies, that man loses his body and leaves behind everything that he had acquired in eighty years.

Whatever we have or acquire in a lifetime is meant to be experienced and taken care of. We have a body through which we connect with the world. We have relationships to experience love, respect and care. We have roles to be played to potential. We have responsibilities to be discharged sincerely. We have wealth to be used in a worthwhile way. Instead of remembering that everything is temporary, we believe it will remain ours forever. Instead of being a trustee, we believe everything 'belongs' to us. Rather than being detached, we get attached and believe it is natural. Instead of enjoying the experience, we live in fear of losing it. Where there is attachment, there is the fear of losing. We fear losing people, positions and possessions. Our deepest fear is of death since the body is the first thing we acquired and our attachment to the body is so strong that we believe the body is 'I'.

Where there is ego, there is attachment. And where there is attachment, there is fear. So, this is an equation worth internalizing:

Ego = Attachment = Fear

The journey of life is not only about accumulating. It also entails using, experiencing and eventually losing them. We lose people, possessions, positions and upon dying, we lose our body too. Death is a juncture where we lose our body and lose everything that we had acquired while we were in that body. But the 'I' never dies, it never gets lost and it has no end. The 'I' simply continues its journey of acquiring, experiencing and losing.

Tell-tale Signs of Ego

Interestingly, we find it easier to recognize ego in other people but not within ourselves. How do we become aware of our own ego, given that we get busy throughout the day and our awareness is always directed at other people? Fortunately, there are certain behaviours which are usually expressive of ego and affirm its presence. These are: arguing, nagging, comparing, complaining, controlling, judging, justifying, accusing, expecting, competing, reacting and so on. A person with ego often has thoughts like these:

- *I like it when everything is about me.*
- *People owe me regard.*
- *I never want to lose the people or the things I like.*
- *What others think of me matters a lot to me.*
- *I want attention, approval, appreciation and acceptance.*
- *I want people to be a certain way.*
- *I want situations to always be favourable.*
- *I cannot handle loss, failures and obstacles.*
- *I want relationships where people support me.*
- *I do not like it when anyone outsmarts me or disagrees with me.*
- *I am not good enough for this.*

Check if you tend to create thoughts similar to these. You are encouraged to do a little inner work to become aware of your ego. This is the process of going outside-in to see where ego is taking shape. Take a moment to do the following:

1. Write down three behaviours (you may choose from the list above) which you relate to.
2. Identify the fear behind each of them.
3. Reflect on the attachment linked to that behaviour.
4. Reason out what it is that you need to let go.

Let us understand with a few examples.

1. **Behaviour: Criticism** - To feel good about ourselves, we often put others down by criticizing them. We snap at people as, 'I do not think your idea is good. It will never work.'
   Fear: 'My idea is better. I am scared that your idea will get accepted.'
   Attachment: 'I identify so closely with my idea. The idea is me.'

2. **Behaviour: Possessiveness** - When we are possessive about someone, our insecurity makes us say, 'I saw you having fun with those people at the party last night.'
   Fear: 'I am scared that you like them more than you like me. What if you leave me?'
   Attachment: 'I am emotionally attached to you. Don't leave me. I cannot live without you.'

3. **Behaviour: Inferiority** - When unable to reach a goal, we forget our worth and hit at our own self-esteem saying, 'I am a failure. I feel like a loser in front of my successful peers.'
   Fear: 'People may ridicule or embarrass me for this failure. Let me withdraw from everyone.'
   Attachment: 'I badly wanted to achieve this goal. It would have earned me respect from my peers and everyone else too.'

4. **Behaviour: Impatience** - Impatience complicates life and makes us unhappy, stressed and anxious individuals who just cannot be in the present. Without considering why other people say or do certain things, we speak in a way

that upsets us and others, such as, 'You are taking too long and that is annoying me. Hurry up.'

Fear: 'If I remain patient, people will take undue advantage and become complacent. Work will get delayed.'

Attachment: 'I will be happy when this gets done, so I cannot wait. I need instant results.'

It is tempting to assume that ego shows up only because we are in the company of other people, getting into interactions and actions with them. If we simply secluded ourselves, withdrew from family and friends, started living alone far away from everyone, will our ego vanish? No. If that happens, we will not know what to do with ego that is already present within us. We will simply continue living with that burden and not know what to change. When someone presses our emotional buttons, we actually get the opportunity to do the inner work of recognizing and getting rid of our ego. So we need to be together with others on this journey of defeating ego.

Ego Consciousness: The Cause of Spiritual Amnesia

'Consciousness' refers to our state of awareness or our belief. Consciousness is like a lens through which we see everything. Our consciousness is the foundation on which we conduct our actions and interactions. As is our consciousness, so will be our intentions, thoughts, perspective, attitude, behaviour, sanskar, personality and hence, destiny. Ego consciousness is also called body consciousness. This is because our physical body is the first thing we acquire in life. Besides, our roles, relationships, positions and possessions exist only as long as we are in the body. The moment we lose the body, we lose all of those too.

What is our consciousness about who we are? The 'I' is inside and we have layer upon layer of all that we have acquired on top of it. This is why we forget the 'I' within. And therefore, we often ponder: 'Who am I? What is the purpose of my life? I have everything but why do I feel so empty within?' We call this spiritual amnesia as we have forgotten the self. When someone loses their memory and forgets who they are, how does their life change? They feel lost, confused, scared and insecure. This happens to us at a spiritual level because we have forgotten who the 'spirit' or 'I' is. Today, we are body conscious. This means:

- If I am in the consciousness of being an Indian, I see people from another country as foreigners.
- If I am in the consciousness of being a CEO, I see the staff in office as my employees.
- If I am in the consciousness of being a servant, I see my employer as my master.

When we are operating out of a consciousness of ego, we interact through the labels and images of our age, role, relationship, position or possessions. Consider three everyday scenarios:

1. In the morning we sternly say to the driver, 'Get the car. Take me to the office. Hurry up.'
2. At office, we say to our boss, 'Sir, kindly approve my leave. I will complete my pending tasks today.'
3. After coming home, we yell at our children, 'Just go to your room, otherwise you will be in trouble.'

Note the difference in our tone, body language, vocabulary and behaviour in each case. We consider this behaviour as normal and that is the reason for anger, irritation and stress, which are also believed to be normal. Ego is like the blanket vice on top of all other emotional disturbances. The moment ego is perceived as normal, then all other negative emotions will also fall into the category of normal. However, once we transcend ego, all other vices are automatically relinquished.

Life in a society calls for certain external hierarchies among people to ensure smooth day-to-day functioning. This is why everyone is assigned a different role, position, relationship and designation. Someone is a president and someone else is a peon. Someone is a mother and someone else is a child. We label the roles and positions 'higher' and 'lower'. But at some point, we get attached to our roles and make them our identity. Higher or lower roles translate into people being treated as superior or inferior, thus creating ego. Let us remember that roles and positions are based on what we achieve by 'doing', according to our intelligence, talent, skill and effort. So it is the roles and positions which are higher or lower, not the people. **Note that ego need not always make us feel superior to someone. It can also make us feel inferior to someone.**

Understanding the Mysterious 'I'

Up until this point, we have answered 'Who am I not?' Now let us come to 'Who am I?' This is a big step towards discovering the truth.

The answer is simple: **I am a soul**.

- I, the soul, am energy called by different names such as the being, spirit, light, power and consciousness.
- I, the soul, am the energy using this body to act and interact.
- I, the soul, am the energy which creates intentions, thoughts, feelings and words.
- I, the soul, am the energy which creates all my relationships.
- I, the soul, am the energy which earns all the possessions and positions along this journey.
- I, the soul, am visualized as a tiny point of divine light shining at the centre of the forehead.

Since the soul is energy, it is not physically visible to the eye. However, one can experience the soul as the energy creating thoughts and taking decisions. The decision is sent to the brain. The brain executes the decision through the body. The body is like a robot which does all the actions, and this robot is controlled by the computer which is the brain. But we know that the computer cannot do anything on its own; it needs an operator. That operator is 'I', the soul.

- Body = Robot
- Brain = Computer controlling the robot
- Soul = Operator of the computer

At times, in our vocabulary, we use expressions such as, 'I have a soul' or 'my soul'. The reality is 'I am a soul and this is my body.' The soul contains all the capabilities: awareness, consciousness, powers, thoughts, feelings and emotions. It is the energy that makes the body function. Our body is the object and the soul gives life to this object.

Know This: You Are Immortal

The law of thermodynamics states that energy can neither be created nor destroyed. And the soul is nothing but energy. So, you are an eternal, indestructible soul. What this means is:

Ether cannot touch you
Wind cannot blow you
Water cannot drown you
Fire cannot burn you
Bullets cannot pierce you
A knife cannot cut you
… and a virus cannot infect you.

Take a moment to let that sink in. And say to yourself: 'There has never been a time when I have not existed, and there will never be a time when I cease to exist.'

The soul and body are symbiotic, so they work together all the time. We are called human beings. 'Human' comes from 'humus', a Latin word for earth or soil, implying that our body is made up of matter (elements). 'Being' refers to the energy, the soul. However, there comes a time when the body ceases to function adequately. That is when the soul leaves the body. When the soul is no longer in the body, we say it is a 'dead body'. Death is for the body and it is a junction where the soul sheds the bodily costume, leaving everyone and everything it had acquired in that lifetime. The soul continues its journey by entering the womb of a mother to take on a new bodily costume, to create new relationships and to play a new role. This is what is referred to as rebirth. So, birth and death are about changing the physical bodily costume as naturally as we change the clothes we wear. We have heard or met children who remember their past lives, which is proof that only the body dies; the one who was living in that body has moved on into a new body. This awareness removes the fear of our own death. This understanding is something to be experienced—when we overcome the fear of death, which is our deepest fear, we are free from many other fears.

There are thousands of stories that people across the world have shared about out-of-body or near-death experiences. This is proof of the soul residing within the body. These are people who were clinically 'dead' but were resuscitated, so the soul left the body for a few moments and then returned into the body. When they are outside the body, few souls can see a clear account of their own life, can look at their own body, see many events and even overhear conversations of people in the vicinity.

Three Aspects of the Soul

The soul, which is a minute spark of energy, is magnificently powerful yet remains undetected by our physical eyes, as it is of a spiritual nature. Medical science can show us the brain. Can it show us our mind? No. Do we need proof that we have a mind? No. We experience it all the time. The soul has three faculties:

- When I, the soul, am thinking, it is called the **mind**.
- When I, the soul, am analysing and deciding, it is called the **intellect**.
- My decision comes into action. Any action done repeatedly, becomes my **sanskar**.

It is similar to how you are one person even when you play the roles of a child, sibling, spouse, parent, friend and so on. The soul is also one energy but it does the work of thinking, of deciding and then of experiencing.

These three faculties of the soul are called the mind, intellect and sanskars respectively. They are not three different energies. They are just one single energy—the soul—performing three functions.

The first alphabets of mind, intellect and sanskar form the acronym MIS. This is comparable to Management Information System, also abbreviated to MIS, which serves as the backbone for any enterprise to run effectively and successfully. Likewise, the MIS trio of the mind, intellect and sanskar play a key role in unfolding our life. There is also a mechanism holding them together to work cyclically. Let us understand each of them.

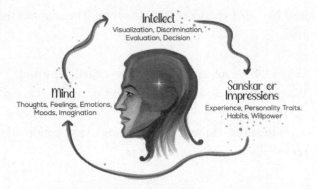

MIS Model of the Mind, Intellect and Sanskars

Mind: A Busy Factory of Thoughts

When the soul is thinking, that faculty is called the mind. The mind and the soul are not separate. In other words, 'mind' is a word we use to address the soul when the soul is thinking. A lot of our experiences are from the world around us—what we see, hear, touch, smell or taste. All these experiences of the external world occur in our mind. We have already understood the workings of the mind in detail. To quickly recap: when you, the soul, are thinking, that is the mind. The mind creates a series of thoughts. In other words, thought is an activity of the mind.

You may recall that the mind creates four types of thoughts. Pure or positive thoughts are selfless and are of love, forgiveness, compassion and empathy. Toxic or negative thoughts are those of ego, anger, malice, laziness and so on. Necessary thoughts are essential ones, relating to our activities. Wasteful thoughts pertain to the past or future or are thoughts about other people's behaviours or situations which we can do nothing about.

Intellect: A Storehouse of Wisdom

Throughout the day, we experience our mind creating multiple thoughts when it comes to making choices: 'Should I go here or should I not?', 'Should I do this or should I not?' This is where the second faculty of the soul, the intellect (called '*Buddhi*' or '*Vivek*' in Hindi), comes into the picture. It is responsible for visualizing, evaluating, discerning and judging the thoughts created by the mind. The mind is like two lawyers putting across two sides of a case. The judge or intellect will listen to both the lawyers. The judge then reasons, discerns and understands before giving a decision. In other words, the intellect decides which thought is to be brought into action and which one is to be discarded. The thought to be acted upon is then transmitted to the brain and we subsequently bring into words or actions.

When you, the soul, are visualizing your thoughts, analysing them and deciding, it is called the intellect. This wisdom, called as the inner voice, intellect, intuition, conscience or gut feeling, is always active and guides us at every step. It is up to us to pay attention, to listen to it and then follow it. If you consider the mind to be a horse, the intellect is akin to the charioteer who holds its reigns. The charioteer controls the horse through the reins. But if the reins are set free by the charioteer, then the horse runs amok. Likewise, the intellect 'tames' the mind so that the mind does not go out of control. But when our intellect is weak, we cannot discern what is right or wrong and what is true or false. Then, the intellect can mislead and give a wrong decision. Just as you do not need evidence that you have a mind, you also do not need proof that you are gifted with an intellect.

Sanskars: Shaping Your Personality

We have understood that our mind creates thoughts and the intellect takes a decision. The decision comes into action. Any action done repeatedly becomes a sanskar. Let us understand the whole picture with the example of an iceberg to put things into perspective. The mind and intellect are the visible parts of the iceberg. This means we are aware of what our mind is thinking at the moment. We are also aware that our intellect is at work when we take decisions and thereafter act upon them. But the 90 per cent of the iceberg that is not visible is the subconscious mind and that is where our sanskars are recorded. We may not use a sanskar but it is nevertheless recorded in the subconscious mind. When a situation comes up, there is a trigger and our thought comes from our sanskar.

For instance, if someone makes a mistake and you get angry at him, you might say, 'I didn't want to get angry but it just happened'. It was a subconscious mechanism that triggered an angry reaction because the sanskar of anger is recorded in the subconscious mind. Millions and millions of our life experiences are stored in the subconscious mind. This is why we do not forget certain incidents. Their recordings are deeply embedded and those memories get triggered when there is a stimulus.

Sanskars refer to personality traits. Gross sanskars are physical habits and ways of doing things such as eating, drinking, sleeping, talking, walking and so on. Subtle sanskars are emotional patterns of thinking and feeling like the habits of caring, sharing, humility, complaining, criticizing, being angry and so on. Any action done repeatedly becomes a sanskar. **Once a sanskar is created, we bypass the first two stages of creating thoughts and then deciding. The sanskar directly comes into action.** That is when we have shifted from a life of awareness to living in 'automatic' mode.

Suppose a person is offered a cigarette for the first time. Here is how his mind, intellect and impressions work:

1. His mind creates two types thoughts: 'Should I smoke? Or should I not?' A chain of deliberations follows: 'Is it okay if I just have one? Nothing wrong in trying once. But it is not good for my health. It might become a habit. But I cannot say no to friends. They might ridicule or reject me. Let me smoke just this once ...'
2. His intellect takes a decision, which will then come into action. Suppose the intellect decides it is fine to smoke just once.
3. He smokes for the first time. Assuming that he experiences relaxation and thrill, those experiences get recorded on the soul as an impression. If his friends cheer him and endorse smoking, that also gets recorded.
4. Suppose he is again offered a cigarette the next week. His mind again creates two thoughts of whether or not to smoke.

5. If his intellect again decides it is fine to smoke, he brings it into action. A second impression of his experience is created on the soul.

6. If this repeats a few times, say ten to fifteen times, the many smoking experiences turn into impressions on the soul. It is like drawing a line with a pencil. Every time we draw, the marking gets darker.

7. After fifteen to twenty times of having decided to smoke, the next time when he is with friends who are smoking or when he is feeling stressed or upset, he is likely to remember the experience of feeling relaxed whenever he smoked in the past. He therefore reaches for a cigarette. The first stage of the mind creating different thoughts is bypassed. Since there are no options in thoughts, the second stage of the intellect taking a decision does even not come into play. This is when smoking becomes his habit.

Just as our mind and intellect work together to form our physical habits, they work to create our sanskars. For instance, suppose a child receives a report card at school and has not scored well. Here is how her mind, intellect and impressions work:

1. She gets frightened of the consequences if she tells her parents the truth. Her mind creates different types of thoughts: 'Should I show my report card at home today? Or should I lie that I have still not got it? But how can I lie to my own parents? They might somehow find out.' More thoughts follow: 'Mummy will surely scold me. What if she

cancels tomorrow's picnic as a punishment? I really do not want to miss the fun.'

2. Her intellect takes a decision to lie to her parents that day, and tell her marks only on the next day after returning from the picnic. That decision comes into action and she lies to them.

3. After a fortnight, suppose she does not complete her assignment, her mind creates two thoughts of whether to fake a headache and get pardoned or to get punished at school.

4. If her intellect decides to tell the truth, she will admit to not doing the homework and get punished by her teacher. But if her intellect again decides that she should lie, she brings it into action.

5. If the girl lies a few more times, maybe on ten to fifteen occasions, then her mind will no longer create two types of thoughts and her intellect will not evaluate or decide. Lying will become her sanskar.

Thereafter, whenever she sees a benefit in lying, she will respond out of that sanskar not only to parents or teachers, but with others too. Effectively, lying becomes a habit and not just a response. Of course, lying becoming a sanskar does not imply that she will lie all the time. After all, honesty is also a sanskar which gets reinforced, each time when she speaks the truth.

Once a sanskar is created, it comes naturally to us. We call it our nature. People often say about their sanskar: 'It is in my genes'. What this means is that it is a sanskar of the soul. Sanskars work on automatic mode. This is the reason for us to believe that we do not choose our emotions and reactions. They simply seem to show up by themselves when there is a situational stimulus. The reaction is not because of the situation, it is because of our sanskar. **A sanskar comes into action automatically. Our reactions, responses, behaviours and habits that come to us naturally are a result of our sanskars.** Most of our sanskars are healthy and beautiful. But we also have a few sanskars that are unhealthy and uncomfortable.

You are encouraged to understand yourself at a deeper level by starting to note down your sanskars.

- Awareness of healthy sanskars will enable you to use them more often. The more you bring them into action, the recordings of those sanskars will get reinforced.
- Awareness of uncomfortable sanskars will enable you to consciously avoid them. When you do not use them, their recordings remain dormant. Importantly, recognizing unhealthy sanskars sets you on a journey of change, which is the very intention of this book.

A Recording with No Retakes

Think of how much care you take before your photo is clicked. Do you know there is an eternal recorder within yourself that is clicking and recording you at every moment? That recording is indelible. And more importantly, there is no retake. **Whatever you think, feel, speak, act on, interact with, read, write, watch, respond and react to—everything that you do in life gets recorded on the soul at every moment.**

In other words, our every karma gets recorded on the soul. The soul recordings remain with us in the present lifetime and get carried forward into our subsequent lives. If we want the recordings to be right, we only need to fix the consciousness. Our consciousness or belief system is the source of our thoughts. It is difficult to check and change the quality of every thought as we create thousands of thoughts every day. But if our consciousness believes 'I am a soul', then we will automatically think right, speak right, work right and live right.

8

Meet the Real 'I'

SUPPOSE YOUR BEST FRIEND HAS SENT YOU A BIRTHDAY present. From the moment you hold it, you cannot stop admiring it. The wrapping paper has an elegant finish and design. There is a pretty-looking silk ribbon bow that perfectly matches the paper, curled and tied across the package. A long note of good wishes is handwritten and stuck just beneath the ribbon. You smile in anticipation of what the gift could be, as you carefully unwrap it. You then find an exotic velvet box with traditional motifs on it. You hold it in your hand and are absolutely enamoured by its beauty. The wow factor makes you believe that the velvet box is your gift. You find the best spot for it on your desk, place it gently and keep gazing at it.

An hour later, your friend calls up to ask if you liked the gift. You thank her profusely for the box. She is somewhat irked when you keep praising the box and the packing. She finally says, 'All that is fine, but tell me about the actual gift. Did you like it?' You have no idea what she is asking. Surprised at your ignorance, she asks you to open that box and look within. Spotting a lining of the lid on the box, you carefully lift it up. The box gets opened and you find the actual gift—a sparkling diamond perfectly set in a pendant. How elated would you feel?

Somehow, this is the way we have lived our lives. We are so thrilled with all the glamour and beauty around us that we fail to discover the diamond within—the actual 'I'. Let us take a moment to unpack our life's most valuable gift. Visualize this scene on the screen of your mind. Look at your designation, position, status and achievements. They are labels and the ribbons in your life: extremely valuable and attractive. Just for a minute, remove them and keep them aside. Next, gently keep aside all that you have bought to use in your life to make your body comfortable and to experience joy through your sense organs. They represent the wrapping paper. Now, you have reached the velvet box that symbolizes your healthy, attractive and extremely useful body. Open that velvet box and you will find a glittering and flawless piece of diamond. **This precious diamond within signifies the real you, the soul residing within the body.**

But why is the awareness of 'I' as a soul so important? Imagine spending a lifetime believing that the gifts of life are the box and the packaging, while remaining oblivious to the diamond inside. Then imagine looking for diamond outside, believing it is too expensive for you to afford. Soul consciousness makes the actual diamond—the innate gifts of purity, love, peace, happiness, power, wisdom and bliss—an eternal reality for every human being. And yet, we imagine these emotions are not always accessible.

You enter a shopping mall and start looking around. Just a few metres away, you find a toddler walking around playfully with her mother. You see her smiling and waving randomly at strangers. As you continue to witness her activities, she accidentally gazes at you and flashes a smile. How does that make you feel? Her vibrations of happiness, purity, innocence, unconditional love and acceptance instantly attract you. You reciprocate by waving back and smiling. During those moments, you forget any stress or problems you have and feel relaxed. This is because you have met a pure, egoless soul. In other words, that child has not yet acquired the wrapping paper, the ribbons and labels and hence has not created the layers of ego that conceal the diamond within. The diamond is exposed, in the sense that the soul's purity radiates to you and attracts you. The same happens in the company of saints as well because, with years of meditation and through other spiritual endeavours, they are closer to their original, soul conscious state.

Although you feel you are experiencing the purity and peace of that child or saint, you actually experience your own purity, which is triggered by their soul consciousness. Their vibrations make you comfortable because they connect you to your own innate beautiful qualities. In other words, the company of a child or a saint brings you the closest to being your pure and peaceful self. On the other hand, the vibrations of ego or body consciousness in one person triggers ego in another. If you meet someone who is body conscious, you also start feeling superior, inferior, angry, scared or insecure.

Ego Consciousness: The Discriminator

Consciousness is like a lens we wear mentally and that lens dictates how we see the world. **Consciousness refers to what we believe about ourselves, others and the world itself.** This is why we do not see anything objectively. We see everything through our beliefs about them. We build their image in our mind and then try to impose that image on them. Forgetting our true identity as souls, we have created ego, which means we have worn the lens of ego consciousness. The lens of ego does not let us identify ourselves as equal souls. It has made us constantly feel superior, inferior, better or worse in reference to each other.

For instance, if we believe we are a role, we connect to another person as a role. That person may have the virtues of kindness and compassion but since we are looking through the lens of role consciousness, we do not see them as a kind and compassionate soul. Our ego consciousness (role consciousness, in this case) will make us see them as a role and hence we will feel either inferior or superior to them. This blocks our energies of respect, acceptance and love. Emotions associated with ego, such as aggression, intolerance, hatred and retaliation get triggered more often. So it is important to wear the right consciousness lens, one that is true and fair for everyone. Today, if we look at our personal life, interpersonal relationships, nation or the world, the root cause of every issue or problem is ego consciousness. Notice our thoughts and feelings as we make these statements and observe how our perspective narrows down on so many levels.

I am an Indian meeting an American.	Nationality consciousness
I am a Hindu talking to a Christian.	Religion consciousness
I am the only woman working with a team of five men.	Gender consciousness
I am older to her so she must obey me.	Age consciousness
I am a father advising my son.	Relationship consciousness
I am a security guard greeting my boss.	Position consciousness
I am a wealthy individual who engages in charity.	Wealth consciousness
I am a landlord, renting my apartment to tenants.	Possession consciousness
I am a pure soul working with another pure soul.	Soul consciousness

All of them (except for the last row) represent different forms of ego consciousness. Ego consciousness is separating us from others through different labels and it is driving us to achieve selfish motives. It is not letting us unite and live in harmony. Reread the last row of the table. Stating 'I am a pure soul' might sound unusual at first, as it is not a part of your day-to-day vocabulary and is not embedded into your consciousness. Maybe you are not sure how this works practically. Do not worry about that. Simply feel the thought for now. You may close your eyes, think of the significant people in your life and then say this line for you and for them:

'I am a pure soul living (or working) with this pure soul.' This line reflects soul consciousness.

Soul Consciousness: The Leveller

Each of us is a soul. Visualize in the centre of the forehead the energy, the flawless diamond.

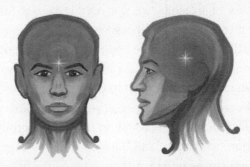

Pictorial Representation of the Seat of the Soul

Say this to yourself slowly:

I am a soul ... the consciousness ... the energy ... the power.
I am a soul ... a tiny point of divine light in the centre of the forehead.
I am a soul ... master of this body.
I am a soul ... I create intentions, thoughts, and feelings.
I am a soul ... I decide my words and behaviours.
I am a soul ... I create my relationships.
I am a soul ... I create my destiny.

The soul cannot be seen or touched; nor can its existence be proven scientifically. **The seat of the soul is in the centre of the brain, between the hypothalamus and pituitary gland.** However, it can be visualized as a point of light at the centre of the forehead. The soul is also called the 'Third Eye of Wisdom'. In Indian culture, a tilak is applied on the forehead, between the eyebrows. That is a reminder of who we are. Besides, in certain places of worship, we not only leave our footwear outside the premises but we also leave leather belts or handbags outside. Leather symbolizes the body, so this practice reminds us to keep our body consciousness away, set ourselves in a soul conscious state and then connect to God, the Supreme Soul.

When we are searching for peace, love and happiness, what we are really looking for is a way to live meaningfully with all of creation, with unity and harmony. This is where soul consciousness comes into play. It operates on the principle of truth, equality and unity. It lets us radiate respect to every soul for who they are and regard them for their age, relationship and position. Soul consciousness recognizes that the other soul has been on a long journey of birth and rebirth, has faced a broad spectrum of situations and hence has created a vast variety of sanskars in response to them. This understanding creates acceptance, compassion, empathy and kindness.

Suppose we say, 'She is five years old'. Whose age is that? The bodily costume is five years old. Before that, the soul probably lived in a costume that was ninety years old, and even prior to that, in yet another bodily costume. But we scold or even raise a hand at the girl only because of perceiving her as a young child. When her bodily costume becomes twenty years old, we say she has grown older, so we do not raise our hand. And when the costume becomes forty years old, we hesitate even to scold her. But if we remember that she is an eternal, wise soul, we will respect the soul even in a five-year-old body. The number we refer to when we say 'my age', is not truly our age. It is the age of the bodily costume we are currently wearing. We are ageless, eternal souls. When we come across a child who is wise beyond the bodily age, we say, 'old soul in a new body' to imply that the child is bringing out the wisdom gained in an earlier lifetime. The truth is that each of us is an old soul in a new body.

Souls Playing Roles

We sometimes complain, 'I am her father but she does not respect me' or 'My housemaid talked back to me today'. When we are in the consciousness of a relationship, we have an image of how the other person should behave. For example, a son should be obedient or an employee should follow instructions sincerely. And if their behaviour does not match this image, our ego gets hurt. It is only when our ego is bruised—which means when someone says or does something that is not as per our expectation of the image we have of them and of ourself—that we get hurt and react.

Society has laid down guidelines for how people are supposed to behave or function depending on their roles. But we routinely find people not complying. At times, we ourselves behave in ways that are unbecoming of us. The knowledge of soul consciousness helps to understand why we deviate: people are not their roles but they are souls playing the roles. Hence, they are bound to behave as per the sanskars of the soul and not always as per the expectations of their role. The film industry is a good example of roleplay. If the same role, script, storyline and movie is offered to different actors, each one will play the role differently. The performance depends on the personality of the actor. The personality of an actor reflects in his role. Similarly, the sanskars and personality of the soul reflect in our various roles and relationships.

When someone in our society does not follow its norms, we must certainly advise, teach, motivate, empower, discipline or request them to inculcate values and sanskars. But at the same time, we should not feel upset or hurt if they do not comply because we know they are a soul on a journey. A soul on the journey of several lifetimes creates a variety of sanskars. We shall understand this in depth in the next chapter. For now, let us know that once the soul creates a sanskar, it lives in an 'automated' mode. The sanskars come in action as the behavioural characteristics associated with the role.

We need to learn to change our uncomfortable sanskars so that, regardless of the role we play—a senior or a junior, the eldest or the youngest, a male or a female—our sanskars of humility, compassion, acceptance and forgiveness prevail every time. Even when our role requires instructing or disciplining someone, we should be able to do it using our sanskars of love and kindness. A versatile movie actor plays any role—that of a pauper or a king, a conman or a cop— equally convincingly and with utmost ease. Whatever may be the role, his personality and style reflect in every scene. Similarly, we need to have awareness in every situation. Remind yourself, 'I, the soul, am playing the role of a parent, spouse and professional. Regardless of the role, my, the actor's personality—of respect, empathy and wisdom should become evident in every scene.' This soul consciousness will make happiness, humility and compassion our natural sanskars and enable us to radiate elevated vibrations and behaviours in every role and every circumstance of life.

Soul consciousness is not just another catchphrase. It is not just a theory, a belief or a fact. And it is not enough to simply believe in it. What is important is to live, experience and practise soul consciousness as we go about our day-to-day lives. To begin with, you may practise two mantras:

- *I am a pure soul.*
- *Everyone I connect with is a pure soul who has been on a long journey and may have acquired sanskars that are different from mine.*

The Three Barriers to Success and Wellbeing

Who in your life is very demanding, to the point that you are fed up of fulfilling their wants? Is it your boss, your spouse, your children ... or life itself? If you think it is any of them, you might want to think again. Nothing and no one is more demanding than our own ego. Ego keeps seeking more and more to keep itself satisfied and pleased. It keeps raising the bar and increasing our expectations of ourselves and others. In fact, other people are also demanding things out of their ego. Expectations, attachments, dependencies, possessiveness and dominance can leave us exhausted. Trying to satisfy ego is a futile struggle, to say the least. Today, many of us have everything that we want externally—physical necessities, comforts, maybe even luxuries. But the 'I' which wants to experience happiness, peace and love is left wanting. This is happening because we are looking for these emotions through consciousness of the body, roles or positions. Let us examine our life when we see ourselves through each of these different consciousnesses: body consciousness, relationship consciousness and role or position consciousness.

Barrier #1: Body Consciousness

We, as souls, want to experience happiness because the nature of the soul is to be happy. When we think we are a body, we try to experience happiness through the body. Therefore, we often make statements like these in pursuit of happiness:

- *Let me listen to good music.*
- *Let me buy this dress.*
- *Let me eat my favourite food.*
- *Let me go on a vacation.*

Make no mistake, each of them is important and add variety to our life experiences. The only mistake is that we add another sentence: 'Let me do this to feel happy.' We want to eat tasty food through the mouth, watch a good movie through the eyes, listen to something exciting through the ears. Basically, when we think we are a body, we try to give happiness to the body through our five sense organs—the eyes, ears, nose, tongue and skin. We all know the feeling. Now, contrast this to buying the things you can afford, the food you can eat, the holidays you can take—do all of these 'happily' rather than 'for happiness'.

It is the nature of the soul to be perfect but we start looking for beauty and perfection in the body. Physical appearance thus starts occupying a lot of our mental space because we look at beauty standards as defined by society and seek to match it. We will therefore want perfect height, ideal weight, expressive eyes, smooth skin, long hair … the list can get both long and unreasonable when we keep comparing our physical appearance with someone else's and measure our self-worth on that basis. It could lead us to create jealousy or hurt. Some of us try to conceal physical imperfections through make-up, cosmetics or even surgeries. The body may not be perfect but we believe we are imperfect. This causes the 'I' to feel inferior or rejected, thus depleting soul power.

Happiness has nothing to do with physical appearance, happiness is all about inner beauty—our intentions, state of mind, character, personality, sanskars and actions. 'I' can be beautiful and perfect even if the body does not match up to the standards of perfection. The innate quality of the soul is happiness but we are trying to experience happiness through money, through the pursuit and purchase of objects. We want to have branded outfits, the best phone, the costliest bike or the latest gadget to feel happier. This is a consequence of our flawed understanding of happiness. It is not a product that can be bought off a supermarket shelf.

Think of a time when you bought an outfit you felt was fashionable, comfortable and suited you well. You wore it to a family event, expecting a compliment or two. But someone remarked that you look old in that outfit. Did you feel bad? Did you start doubting your choice? Did you not like them for saying it? Reflect on this: you are the same person who was happy to wear the outfit of your choice, but now you feel hurt. Your thoughts on buying the new outfit had created happiness, and now your thoughts on receiving criticism have created hurt. Your thoughts are created by the soul (mind), based on your consciousness. When you are soul conscious, perfection in sanskars becomes your priority. You take care of your body as a trustee, keeping it healthy. You buy material objects for physical comfort rather than for happiness. You choose what to experience through the sense organs, thereby gaining mastery over them. You control the objects or gadgets you possess and do not get controlled by them.

Barrier #2: Relationship Consciousness

We often think, speak and behave through the labels of relationships. For instance, we say:

- *I am a teacher. How should my students behave with me?*
- *I am your best friend. You should not hide anything from me.*
- *Is this how a husband should treat his wife?*

Someone having the consciousness of being a father creates certain expectations from a son. For instance, if his son is rude, he says, 'I am his father. How could he talk to me like that especially in front of others?' Let us analyse the scene:

- The father was connecting with his child through the image of how a son should behave with a father.
- The father's expectations were a result of that image. So he wanted the son's behaviour to align with the image of an ideal child: polite and respectful.
- When the son pricked or damaged that image with rudeness or disrespect, the father could not accept it.
- The father felt insulted since he did not receive respect from his son, which he had assumed to be a 'normal expectation' in their relationship.

All of us create a mental image of an ideal parent, child, spouse, friend and colleague. These images are certainly important as they teach us about the right sanskars for us to create. They give us an idea of what to deliver as we play different roles throughout the day. The images we all hold are benchmarks used by us, by the society or by elders in the family, to teach everyone how to be. But in the field of relationships, it helps to remember that everyone cannot live up to that image. In our own experience we would have seen that a few people may come nowhere close to that image, a few people match that image, while a few others do way better than that image, going above and beyond our expectations.

Everyone is a soul on a long journey of multiple lifetimes, so they carry many, many sanskars. This understanding helps us to accept people and respect them, and yet guide and discipline them, thereby helping them create new sanskars. Whenever we connect to each other through the consciousness of the labels of relationships, we are bringing ego into play. Since both of us are attached to a false image of ourselves, it is the ego of one that connects to the ego of the other. Trying to satisfy the ego makes our relationships complicated. Differences of opinion trigger disrespect, arguments or conflicts. That is why the term 'ego clashes' has been coined. When we connect to each other through soul consciousness, then it is a soul-to-soul connection. Soul consciousness helps us understand the other soul's behaviour and have no expectations. It inspires us to enter relationships only to give and not to want anything. It enables us to radiate unconditional love, acceptance and harmony.

You might have experienced soul-to-soul relationships with a few people in your own life. You bond well and accept each other easily. These are your soul connections, where love and care are exchanged effortlessly. You refer to such a person as a 'soul sister' or 'soul brother'. Just by shifting from ego to soul consciousness, we can turn every single relationship into a soul connection.

Let us analyse the earlier scenario of the interaction between a father and son, to understand what difference a soul-to-soul connection would make. Suppose the father is in soul consciousness and the son speaks rudely to him in front of many people. Visualize the scene and the father's response:

- The father does not seek love and respect from his son (or from anyone, for that matter). He experiences love and respect as his own innate nature.
- He is unaffected by the son's rude words. He remains calm and stable internally and externally.
- He understands that his son is in emotional pain for him to be so rude—maybe due to a wrong sanskar being

activated, due to bad mood or owing to some pressure. So he does not create judgemental or critical thoughts.

- The father knows he has the power to heal his son with love. He either remains silent at that moment or assertively (not angrily) tells the son that his behaviour was not right.
- Radiating compassion, love and respect, he empowers his son to understand and change.
- The father remains untouched by the opinions of the other people who witnessed the scene. Being soul conscious, he is not dependent on public approval to feel good. He understands they are entitled to different views according to their sanskars.

Can you see what a vast difference soul consciousness makes to relationships? We live with the illusion that we experience love and respect only when we receive them from people. Love and respect are the inherent qualities of the soul. These emotions are to be experienced from the inside out, and not from the outside in. We experience them only when we radiate them to other people. Once we stop wanting and start giving, we become the first ones to experience these feelings.

Barrier #3: Role or Position Consciousness

When we identify ourselves with a role or position, we believe happiness and respect come from what we achieve, and that power can be experienced when people are in our control. We try to get happiness by rising in ranks, by achieving more and by outperforming others. In the process of achieving more and neglecting self-care, we create stress, aggression, jealousy, insecurity, manipulation and even corruption and the 'I' moves away from power and happiness.

For instance, a CEO speaks out of ego when he says, 'I am your boss. So, you should do exactly as I say.'

The ego of the employee gets triggered. He replies, 'Sir, I certainly respect your position. But I want to execute it my way.'

This is how their egos clash. And then begins a journey of giving each other a hard time, all because of their egos. Their peace of mind, physical health, relationship, the employee's career and eventually, the project itself suffers. Nothing good ever comes out of a clash of egos and the need to satisfy one's ego.

The soul experiences power when it is a master of its mind, and when it can remain untouched by the energy of situations and people's behaviour. Today, since our mind and sense organs are not always under our control, we do not experience the control within us. This is why we want situations and people to be in our control.

Awakening to Soul Consciousness

Visualize this situation as vividly as you can. Suppose you are an employee heading to office in the morning.

- You drive to your office. How do you talk to the security guard?
- You enter the building. How do you talk to the receptionist?

- A team member greets you on the way to your desk. How do you talk to him?
- The CEO passes by, just as you settle down. How do you talk to her?

It is possible that:

- You ignore the guard. You do not even acknowledge his presence.
- The receptionist greets you but you do not reply as you are already thinking of the day's workload. You just nod and walk past her.
- Your team member wants to have a word with you but you cut him off and ask him to send you the project report.
- Your CEO passes your desk. You stand up, greet her and speak softly to her.

'Just be yourself' we are often told. But could you see your behaviour change four times in less than fifteen minutes, as you met the four people? Applying that wisdom here, which of the four behaviours reflect your natural self? The answer is, none of them. Because if something is natural, it would not have changed. The most important question is: why did you change your behaviour four times?

We believe it is normal to conduct ourselves differently with the people around us, especially when interacting with four different roles. We justify that we are responding in a way in which we can relate to them. Notice that the four behaviours appear to be perfect for a role-to-role connection.

Since our consciousness is 'I am the role', we see others also through that consciousness and behave accordingly with them. That is why we do not find the need to smile and greet the security guard. We feel it is not needed for that role. We may believe that we are respecting the CEO. But that may not be authentic. Perhaps we are respecting their position or their achievement. Maybe we want to impress them. Or we possibly want something from them. Let us check our intentions: Are we respecting the person or are we respecting their role? Will we respect them the same way if they lose that position? Are we respecting them only through outward behaviour or do we respect them in our thoughts and feelings also?

Can we not speak with the same dignity and respect to everyone? We can. What stops us is our ego—our attachment to the wrong image of being superior, inferior, better than or not as good as someone. When we are talking to a security guard, or to our driver or peon, if we are conscious of their role, then we expect them to be respectful but we do not feel the need to be equally respectful to them. If they make a mistake, we believe we have the right to shout at them but if we make a mistake, we believe they must keep quiet. These are beliefs that are created based on role consciousness. We will be ourselves and interact with others through our true nature only when we are talking person to person, a soul connecting to another soul.

Going back to the earlier example, visualize yourself being in soul consciousness. You head to the office and meet the same four people. You are likely to respond this way:

- As you enter the gate, you respectfully smile at the soul playing the role of the security guard.
- You acknowledge and reciprocate the greeting of the soul playing the role of the receptionist.
- You listen calmly to the soul playing the role of your colleague and respond in a friendly manner.
- You stand up to give regard to the soul playing the role of your CEO but your tone and behaviour do not change. Your respect for her does not increase based on the role she is playing.

When we are aware of being a soul playing a role, ego clashes, power games, short-term financial gains, achievements at the cost of our health and relationships will all appear insignificant. We will see others also as equal souls. Our nature will not change four times.

You may ask: How is it possible to behave in the same manner with the CEO and the security guard? Our behaviour is a combination of two aspects: respect and regard. Respect is internal. It is in our consciousness, our belief about the identity of the individual, our thoughts and feelings and the vibrations we radiate. Regard is external. It is in our behaviour. We will examine this more closely in the next section. Your behaviour can change because you need to give regard according to people's roles. For instance, you do not need to come out of your car to greet the security guard. If he salutes you, you do not have to salute him in return. But your consciousness remains the same: one of equality. Respect is for the soul; regard is for the role. Regard can be different; respect will be the same for all.

In ego consciousness, when you feel superior, the other person feels inferior. When you feel inferior, the other person feels superior. This is because your consciousness also takes them into the consciousness of their role—or they may already be in the consciousness of their role. But when you are in soul consciousness, connecting to each one as an equal, you are in an egoless state. Your consciousness influences the other person and they also shift to being themselves. This is a soul-to-soul connect, having a vibration of equality, humility and acceptance.

Ego consciousness may have become the default today but soul consciousness is our true essence. Soul consciousness is natural for all of us. Let us keep practising it each day. We may tend to fall back into body consciousness time and again. But as soon as we notice, the act of noticing itself nudges us back to soul consciousness. The process can be a gradual one because we are shifting from 100 per cent ego consciousness to 100 per cent soul consciousness. Expecting instant results would be wishful thinking. It is comparable to watching a plant grow. We do not sit in front of it all day and stare at it. We simply water it every day. It takes a few days or weeks to spot a new branch or a new leaf. Likewise, we just need to nurture the self every day. After a few days we will be able to notice changes in our thoughts and behaviour. So let us never think, 'This transformation is difficult. Soul consciousness is not possible in practical life … when everyone else is not doing it how can I do it?' These thoughts create a barrier in our journey of transformation.

The more we remind ourselves that we are souls, the easier it becomes to shift towards soul consciousness.

Let us practise soul consciousness in every scene:

- While doing every task, create the thought, 'I, the soul, am doing this'.
- Before meeting someone, create the thoughts, 'I am a pure soul meeting another pure soul. We will have a beautiful meeting today'.
- If you find it hard to accept someone's sanskars or behaviour, create the thought, 'I am a powerful soul. I understand them. This soul has created this sanskar on the journey of life'.

Practising soul consciousness is similar to the experience of watching a movie or a play. While watching, you are aware that the cast is comprised of actors playing their roles. You do not get entangled in the roles that they are portraying. You appreciate the actors playing different roles for their performances. The actor is the soul or the 'being', while the role reflects the 'doing'.

Can You Respect Everyone Equally?

The answer is: Yes.

Respect is an internal feeling created for a soul, for who they are. Since we are all equally pure, equally beautiful and equal beings, respect should not vary from person to person. Every individual is to be equally and uniformly respected. It has nothing to do with their age, role, status or achievements. Respect implies acceptance, which means the energy flowing from us to the other person remains pure. Our thoughts and words about them are always right. We interact with them with equality and dignity. We like their qualities, their behaviour and their karmas. Even when we disagree with their views or sanskars, we do not question their ways. We empathize that the soul has created that sanskar due to certain situations on its journey of many lifetimes. We also understand that people can be and do things only as per their qualities, views and capacities. But if we get disturbed because of people's sanskars, it means we are first disrespecting ourselves. We react impulsively and thus disrespect the other person too. When our self-respect is high, we can accept others easily. Thereafter, respecting them becomes natural.

On the other hand, regard can vary from one person to another. **Regard is an external courtesy or protocol extended according to the roles, relationships, age, position, knowledge, status and achievements of people.** Therefore, it need not be uniform for everyone. Regard is a vital component in the way we relate to other people and is reflected in our behaviour. For instance, when a student receives a medal for topping the class, the other students clap and applaud her. This is a regard given for her hard work and achievement. Another example of regard is where everyone at home takes blessings from the eldest member of the family, before heading out each morning. This is a regard given for seniority in age and relationship. Other examples of showing regard are: listening actively, waiting for our turn to speak, giving up our seat or holding a door open for someone.

In a school, students stand up to greet the teacher when she enters. They maintain silence when the teacher begins the lesson. This is regard given by students for the teacher's role. The same school has a peon but students do not need to stand up to greet the peon or offer their chair to him. However, can the students talk to the peon equally lovingly and respectfully like they talk to their teachers? Yes, they can. We even see that happen.

Having understood the difference between regard and respect, think about this:

- **Can you extend regard without giving respect?**

  Yes, you can. At times, you speak politely and do exactly what the other person says. But while doing it, if you are critical or judgemental about them, it means you are not radiating respect in those moments. You are internally disrespectful but are extending regard, maybe due to their seniority in position, achievements or bodily age.

- **Can you respect someone even if you do not meet their expectations?**

  Yes, you can. Has anyone told you, 'If you respect me, do this for me' or snapped at you, saying, 'You couldn't even do that much. You do not respect me'? Our feelings for people and what we do for them are separate entities. You may genuinely respect someone, yet not be able to do everything that they expect from you. On the other hand, you may obey every word that someone says merely out of compulsion or helplessness but internally you disrespect that person. So it is important that we never equate respect for someone with meeting their expectations. We have the power to adjust, adapt, stretch our comfort zones, change our sanskars, to meet someone's expectations. But it is important that we do it with love and respect, and not out of compulsion or frustration or fear. Otherwise, we may not be happy but still be doing it, and thereafter we expect them to return the favour. Therefore, we need to keep talking to the self, till we come to the answer: 'I am doing it because I choose to do it. I am doing it willingly for myself, not for them.'

Dismantling Gender Stereotypes

We explored various labels assigned to ego or body consciousness. One of them happens to be gender. Our gender, when perceived as an identity rather than as the physiology of our body, leaves a significant impact in the way we think, feel, behave or experience our lives. Today, it is playing a huge role even in the way others perceive us. However, it helps to understand that gender applies only to the body and not to the soul. One person is clad in a sari, and someone else wears a T-shirt and jeans. In a similar way, we are all souls but the bodily costume we wear is different. Someone is in a male costume and another is in a female costume. On a journey of many births, each of us would have been in male and female costumes. The gender which keeps changing is for the body and not the soul.

Qualities or personality traits are attributes of the soul and have nothing to do with the gender of the body. However, society has been conditioned to believe and live otherwise. Certain personality traits and qualities have been traditionally associated with the masculine gender and certain others with the feminine gender. This conditioning helps to lay down specific attributes, responsibilities or roles for men and women in a society. But stereotyping certain traits as 'imperative', which must be performed or possessed only by men or only by women just because of their gender, is questionable. It has led to wrong notions and harmful consequences in the way individuals are raised, perceived or treated. It has even limited people's capacity to rise to their full potential and has affected their fundamental freedom such as rights to health, education, career, relationships and so on. Let us consider a few examples:

- **Traits perceived as feminine**: Powerful (resilient), compassionate, nurturing, graceful, gentle, mild, understanding, intuitive.
- **Traits perceived as masculine**: Strong (physical endurance), aggressive, authoritative, adventurous, competitive, analytical.

Professional roles like that of doctors, entrepreneurs or lawyers require inculcating specific personality traits or sanskars to experience more success. Society seems to apply similar guidelines for the roles men and women play. Historically, men and women had clearly demarcated duties. A man's role based on gender was to earn money, support the family and be the breadwinner for the household. A woman's role was that of a nurturer and a caregiver for the family, handling all the household chores. Accordingly, boys and girls were conditioned to imbibe those sanskars. As they were used more frequently, those sanskars became more activated or dominant in their personality. This led to a misconception that each gender excels only at specific roles.

In daily life, we see that sanskars cannot be stereotyped based on gender. The extent of a particular trait within us depends on our sanskars, past experiences and social conditioning. This is why we sometimes find men who are more caring and compassionate than women. Likewise, we come across women who are more daring or outspoken than their male counterparts. This goes to show that qualities or traits are not decided by biological gender.

If you wear a blue outfit and your friend wears a white one, will you feel superior or inferior to him? You do not. You understand it is just a matter of wearing different clothes. The same applies to a bodily costume. A soul who has taken a male bodily costume is not superior to a soul who has taken a female costume. Superiority and inferiority are mere constructs created and sustained by the society based on certain roles. As per this construct, the provider was believed to be superior and the nurturer was dependent on the provider in the past. So women were denied several rights and opportunities.

Women today are just as they were in the past. How are they now able to shine in every role today? How are they able to take any challenge in their stride? What led to such staggering changes in their ways? Turns out that sanskars are the answer—sanskars are not gender-specific. They are simply soul-specific. A woman has always had the sanskars needed to progress in the professional and public domains, just as her male counterparts have. It was only a matter of a woman using those sanskars or not. In the past centuries, a woman had limited or no avenues to bring those sanskars into action. So, the sanskars remained dormant—they were present but rendered inactive. Today, she has opportunities to bring those sanskars to the fore and strengthen them further.

Women need to remember they are neither inferior nor superior to men. **All souls are equal but different, based on their sanskars**. They need not compare or compete to prove themselves. They need not do anything that does not align with their sanskars and principles, just to prove they are on par with men in the various roles they play. Both men and women need to focus on their own sanskars and elevate their vibrations. The need of the hour is to strengthen 'who we are' while excelling at 'what we do'.

Sanskars are about the soul, never about the gender. In the next chapter, we shall explore why a soul has a particular set of sanskars, why our sanskars differ and how these sanskars are created.

Sustaining Self-Awareness

We set out on the journey of knowing 'I am a soul' and now we have set a goal of making soul consciousness our natural way of living. With awareness and a little attention, we can experience it and gradually remain in that state even while playing all our roles and doing everything that needs to be done. When we start reminding ourselves every morning, before beginning a task, before every meeting, during every interaction and before sleeping at night, that we are souls, slowly the duration of the soul conscious stage will increase. Transformation from body consciousness to soul consciousness may happen in small steps but is nevertheless a huge achievement. Even a slight shift will have a multifold effect on how we experience life. Pause and feel how your egoless state would be: egoless in relationships, egoless at work, egoless all the time and the soul sparkling like a flawless diamond. Just thinking and visualizing it feels divine, doesn't it?

9

Your Ever-changing Personality

H AVE YOU SAT IN A PARK AND WATCHED PEOPLE AROUND
you for about an hour? You often get to witness
interesting scenes unfold. A person picks up a piece of trash
and throws it in the bin, someone helps a child get on and
off a swing, someone else lends water to a person who is
coughing, another person smiles when you make eye contact,
somebody watches over a child whose parent is on a phone
call … you come across plenty of good deeds.

But just as you start appreciating the benevolent and
generous human spirit, you overhear conversations of an
opposite quality from multiple people. They vent to each
other about a family member or a neighbour or a colleague—
narrating how someone was being mean, taking advantage,
betraying, causing harm, obstructing success, disrespecting
and so on. These stories do not end well, do they?

We humans have a sense of unity and cooperation, but we also seem to be getting more divisive than ever. Our beautiful sanskars are on display but so are the harmful ones. We have the capacity to love, care, forgive and accept each other, but we have been criticizing, retaliating, blaming and rejecting as well. If being nice is normal, why is morality collapsing right before our eyes? And if not being nice is normal, why do we routinely come across acts of kindness?

Are People Normally Good or Bad?

Give this a thought: eight billion of us on the planet are expressing our nature through our sanskars throughout the day, impacting each other either positively or negatively. So it is important to know:

- Did we start our life with right sanskars and then pick up wrong sanskars along the way?
- Did we start with wrong sanskars and then create right ones?
- Did we start with a blank slate and then create both right and wrong sanskars?
- Do we all have a common ground when it comes to our sanskars?

Look at your own life. What triggers your sanskars? How do you acquire a sanskar? Is it genetic? Is it through the nurturing you have received? Is it from your environmental influences? Does it come from someone you idolize and emulate? Or is it a combination of these factors? We know we are prone to creating both healthy and unhealthy sanskars but how we get to that point is interesting. After all, once a sanskar is formed, the mind does not create thought options and the intellect does not need to take a decision. We do not choose what to think, what to speak, how to behave or what action to take. That sanskar gets triggered automatically.

The Five Blueprints for Your Sanskars

We, as souls, are nothing but a bundle of our sanskars. Our personality is a combination of five types of sanskars. Just as there are folders on a computer, we have five folders of sanskars recorded on the soul. Each folder has different sanskars.

Here are the five folders or sets of sanskars that make us who we are:

- **Set 1:** Sanskars we have carried from our past lifetimes
- **Set 2:** Sanskars received from parents and family, called hereditary sanskars
- **Set 3:** Sanskars created due to environmental influences
- **Set 4:** Sanskars created through our willpower
- **Set 5:** Our innate, original sanskars

Recognizing sanskars helps us understand our own behavioural patterns as well as other people's behaviours.

Set 1: The Sanskars of Your Past Births

- A four-year-old plays the piano effortlessly.
- A five-year-old fluently recites verses from a scripture.
- A seven-year-old writes complex software code.

Surprisingly, their families are often neither inclined nor trained in these areas. So everyone wonders, 'When and how did this young child learn this skill?'

Now we know the truth. These children are not four years or six years old. They are old souls in a four-year-old or a six-year-old body in this birth. Previously, these souls were in different bodily costumes. You may recall from the previous chapter that the soul is energy and energy cannot be destroyed. So, a soul never dies; it is eternal. When the body ceases to function, the soul leaves the body. And as per its karmic patterns, the soul enters the womb of a mother during the early stage of pregnancy.

Till the age of about two to three years, a child (soul) has memories of past life. This is why we find a few children recalling memories from their past life. But as layers of information of the present life get formed, the past life memories fade and eventually get forgotten. Of course, only the facts fade but the sanskars continue to remain on the soul.

Do We Come Empty-Handed?

Visualize the journey of the soul. A soul in a body for 100 years creates many sanskars and develops several talents and skills. One day, the soul leaves the body and everything is left behind. We often hear or say, 'We come into this world empty-handed and we leave empty-handed'. However, this is not true. At a physical or material level, this statement is valid since we neither bring anything with us when we are born, nor do we take anything with us when we leave the body. Our physical possessions are left behind. But we, the souls, do not leave empty-handed. The soul changing a body is like us changing our outfit or costume. When we change our costume, we as a person do not change. Only our outfit changes. When a soul leaves a body and takes another one, it will remain the same soul having the same nature and the same sanskars as before.

Picture a soul in an eighty-year-old body: suppose the personality and sanskars of this soul are of being caring, kind, humble, fearful, anxious and getting hurt easily. Also, let us assume this soul has deep knowledge of the scriptures and imparts that knowledge to students. Suppose that soul leaves the body when the body is 100 years old. What does the soul carry with it? All these sanskars. And along with these sanskars, the soul enters the womb of a mother. The baby born after a few months is therefore not a new soul. It is an old soul in a new body. Also, the soul is not a clean slate or a blank CD, so to say. It already has sanskars recorded from the previous birth. By the time the new body turns three years old, how will his nature be? The child will be caring, kind, afraid of being alone and will start crying when he does not get what he wants. That child may also display an avid inclination towards the scriptures and perhaps starts repeating them from memory, much to the amazement of people around him. They may not understand that the past sanskars carried by the soul are playing out.

Let us understand this with an analogy:

- Look at it like a recording of several songs (sanskars) on a CD (soul), playing on a CD player (body) today.

> - Tomorrow, the CD (soul) can be removed from this player (body) and inserted into another CD player.
> - It is important to note that the CD (soul) still carries the same songs (sanskars). Only the player has changed but the songs do not get deleted.

The eternal journey of the soul continues—from one costume to another, one lifetime to another. In each costume, that soul gets a different set of parents, environments, culture, situations, experiences and therefore creates several different sanskars. All our sanskars, including those of our past lives, are recorded in the subconscious mind. These sanskars get triggered when a situation comes up.

One Understanding to End All Misunderstandings

- *How can you behave this way?*
- *I can never understand you.*
- *You are completely different from the rest of us in the family.*

Many of us either say or hear such statements, especially when someone's sanskars do not match ours. We often fail to understand people as we see them in their present costume and do not realize they are carrying a past. Looking at them through the label of relationships and roles, we set expectations of how our parents, spouse, child, friends, peers and boss should be.

People are not their roles or relationships. Every person is a soul. The journey of a soul is not limited to the present lifetime but includes experiences and sanskars of past lives too. This understanding simplifies and strengthens our relationships. Take a moment to look at your family members. Each of them is a soul on a long journey. We do not know—even they do not know—what experiences they have been through that have shaped them into who they are today. Each one has beautiful sanskars as well as a few uncomfortable sanskars. You can help people change their wrong sanskars—we shall understand the process shortly. But the first step towards a change is accepting their sanskars. Acceptance comes from understanding the soul's journey. We may not agree or approve of their sanskars but we understand why they are carrying them.

When You Are Different from Your Family

A four-year-old child attending kindergarten classes steals her friend's pencils. Her parents cannot comprehend why she steals when they have provided her the best of comforts. Moreover, they have taught her to be honest. What they do not realize is that their daughter also does not know why she steals. She has carried the sanskar of stealing from a past birth.

Parents typically believe that children come into their world with no previously recorded sanskars. They mentally prepare a long list of beautiful sanskars to inculcate in their child. They visualize their child bringing those sanskars into action: happy, respectful, calm, honest, sincere, hardworking, polite and resilient. But that child is not a fresh soul and will not come with a clean or blank CD of sanskars. The child carries several past-life sanskars. At times, it may turn out that the child has sanskars opposite to that of the parents. For example:

- Parents are honest and ethical but the child lies even over trivial issues.
- Parents are perfectionists but the child is careless.
- Parents are exceptionally organized but the child is clumsy.
- Parents are punctual but the child is always behind schedule.

Of course, the opposite is also true:

- Parents are manipulative but the child is honest.
- Parents are lazy but the child is diligent.
- Parents exaggerate matters but the child tells the truth.
- Parents worry easily but the child remains calm.

Parents often express shock or awe at how their child can be so different. Sometimes they criticize or compare their child with others. This radiates rejection, which means disrespect for the soul. The repeated nagging disempowers the soul and so the child might refuse to change. Even if the child wants to change a sanskar, the soul lacks power to do so.

While parents are still in the process of understanding their child's sanskars, let us say another soul—their next child— enters their lives. This soul also carries many sanskars from past lifetimes. This means both the children carry different past sanskars into this birth. Typically, the parents not only compare the children's sanskars with their own, but also start comparing their two children with each other. It surprises many parents, who say, 'I have given the same upbringing to both my children, yet why are they so different?' Parents of identical twins often wonder, 'Both were born at nearly the same time, went to the same school, have the same set of friends, grew up in the same environment ... yet why are they are so different?'

When interacting with children, parents typically perceive them as a one-year-old, ten-year-old or a twenty-year-old. When we see the child as being young, we take the liberty to scold or even physically punish them in the name of discipline. But the ages denote only the duration the soul has spent in this particular physical costume or the body.

A Shift From the Three Cs to the Three As

Soul consciousness prompts us to give up the **Three Cs: Criticism, Comparison** and **Control**, and adopt the **Three As: Acceptance, Approval** and **Appreciation**. Shifting from body consciousness or role consciousness to soul consciousness magically transforms how parents understand their children. Soul consciousness changes the very style of parenting. When we do this not just with children but with every soul, all our relationships start thriving.

Consider an example scenario where the parents are national-level swimmers. They dream of their daughter also becoming a champion swimmer. However, that child detests the very idea of going anywhere near a pool, let alone taking swimming lessons. Confused and disheartened, the parents scold her to get over the fear of water. But if the parents become aware that their daughter, who is a soul on a journey, had left the body because of a flood in her previous lifetime, how would they respond? Suppose they come to know that in the final moments of her past life, that soul had witnessed her own self, family, friends, neighbours and house—all getting washed away in a flood. Will the parents continue criticizing her for fearing water in the present life? Not at all. They will empathize with her fear and admit, 'Obviously our daughter will be terrified about getting into a swimming pool'. When they realize that her fears stem from a past life experience, they will be able to guide her gently to overcome the fear and eventually learn to swim. What seemed unnatural to believe when they saw her as a daughter of swimmers becomes easy to accept when they see the journey of the soul.

An understanding of the eternal soul journey makes acceptance easy and natural. Acceptance radiates respect and power to the soul. Acceptance does not mean they let the sanskar be, even if it is uncomfortable. Acceptance makes way to respectfully help people change wrong sanskars. The focus should be on the creation of new sanskars, not finishing the old ones. As a soul uses the new sanskar more often, the old ones will fade away.

When You Cannot Understand, Accept

Several couples spend a lifetime trying to change each other, arguing: 'Why are you like this? Why can't you be like me?'

The two souls are like two CDs consisting of two completely different sanskar recordings. What are these people essentially doing? They are expecting the other CD to have the same songs as theirs. They are trying to match the songs on the CDs or trying to overwrite each other's songs. Let alone being fair, it is not even realistic. The journey, experiences and emotions are going to be different for different souls, in just a twenty-four-hour span. How different will our journey be over an entire lifetime? And how vastly different will it be across several lifetimes? Yet, we have grown up believing expectations are natural, which means expecting the other soul to have the same sanskars as ours is natural. How can it be natural for them to be able to understand our sanskar or for us to understand theirs?

Does it mean we cannot understand each other? Let us not try to understand other people's sanskars. To understand someone's sanskar, we need to have the same sanskar as they do. So an easier solution is to accept people's sanskars. Acceptance does not mean we let a wrong sanskar be the way it is. Acceptance only means that we realize that sanskar was created by that soul due to certain circumstances in their present or a past lifetime. Acceptance means we do not condemn, criticize, compare or question why they are the way they are. Such acceptance strengthens us and empowers them. A powerful soul can change any sanskar, regardless of how old or rigid it is.

Set 2: Your Hereditary Sanskars

The second set of sanskars we receive is from immediate family like parents, siblings, grandparents and other relatives like uncles or aunts. They constantly nurture us to be a certain way, about how we should speak, eat, behave, interact and treat others. They try to inculcate in us the habits they want us to develop.

- *I must have got my friendly gene from my dad.*
- *I am an introvert just like both my parents.*
- *They say I am as short-tempered as my grandpa.*

Have you said or heard such statements? It is common for people to attribute certain characteristics in their personality—sanskars, inclinations, behaviours, virtues and even weaknesses—to family members, terming them as 'natural' or 'obvious'. During formative years, the absorption power of children in terms of what they hear, see and feel is extremely high. This is because children are soul conscious and do not have rigid ideas about life.

Sanskars of a family are not only taught to a child but also radiated. In other words, a child absorbs sanskars when elders live by those sanskars. Irrespective of whether the sanskar is in the behaviour of the adults or is only in their intentions and thoughts, the child catches the vibrations. **Sanskars cannot be passed on to children without parents living by them.** If parents preach a particular sanskar but practise something else, then the child receives a contradictory energy. For instance, if parents are rude and harsh to their cook and driver but teach their child to be respectful towards everyone, then the child finds it confusing. A child does not live in body or ego consciousness and hence cannot understand roles. Therefore, the child cannot comprehend the parents' behaviour.

It is important for parents, family and teachers to live the right sanskars—not only in the presence of children, but even while they are away. When parents live a sanskar, it becomes a part of their vibration and children absorb those vibrations. So the parenting equation is straightforward:

- Want your child to be cheerful? Be happy yourself.
- Want your child to be honest? Practise sincerity.
- Want your child to be respectful? Be courteous with everyone.
- Want your child to have strong self-respect? Remain untouched by peer pressure.

The mantra for parenting is: just BE what you want your children to be.

Principles of Garbh Sanskar (Womb Psychology)

At what age do you believe you started getting sanskars from your parents? At three years, one year—or from the day you were born?

The answer is: even before you were born.

Sanskars begin to take shape while a soul is in the womb. Research in birth psychology, the science behind Garbh Sanskar, has evidence that parents have the power to influence the sanskars and thereby the destiny of their child from the moment a soul enters the mother's womb. A soul in the womb implies there are two souls in the same body. So both souls are influenced by each other's vibrations. Therefore, an expectant mother experiences changes in her emotions, habits, food preferences and, in general, some of her likes and dislikes during pregnancy. The soul which has entered her womb is influencing her. However, it is the mother's mind which has the strongest influence on the child's mind. A baby is in a 'detached' state in the womb as it is not yet emotionally attached to its new body, people or environment. So that soul has a greater ability to catch vibrations from the surroundings. Like a sponge, that baby absorbs the thoughts, feelings, visuals, sounds and behaviours from the vicinity. Whatever the parents think, feel, watch, speak or listen to is what the baby absorbs and becomes.

Like the physical health of the mother is important for the physical wellbeing of the child, good emotional health of parents also goes a long way in ensuring the emotional and mental wellbeing of the child. This makes it imperative for parents to:

- Release negative emotions like anger, hurt, worry, fear, jealousy, stress or guilt.
- Let go of past hurt and make forgiveness a natural way of living.
- Stay away from negative conversations like gossip, judgements, arguments and fights.
- Use high vibrational words in every conversation.
- Avoid content that depict pain, fear, violence, aggression, hatred or sorrow. Consume pure, empowering spiritual content to nurture the child emotionally.

- Whatever may be the situation, think right. This builds emotional resilience of the child.
- Make the sanskars of purity, peace, love, compassion, happiness and humility a natural way of being. This sows the seeds of virtues in the personality of the child.
- Refrain from having gender preferences, or fears and doubts about your parenting ability. The child might otherwise feel unwanted and carry the feeling of being rejected for years.
- Adhere to a Satvik (vegetarian) fresh diet, prepared and consumed in a pure state of mind and clean environment. You are what you eat and your child is becoming what you eat, emotionally and physically.
- Practise meditation and visualization exercises.

Set 3: Sanskars Created Due to Your Present Environment

- *I was lazy but my friend's success inspired me to work hard.*
- *I was so nervous to speak but my teacher instilled confidence in me.*
- *He has completely changed after relocating to that country.*
- *There are so many artists in her family. She naturally paints well.*

Have you heard similar statements or stated them yourself? Parental and familial influence have a significant bearing in the formation of our sanskars but environmental factors are just as substantial. 'You are as good as the company you keep' is a popular expression for a reason. Environmental influences in terms of the people around us—their beliefs, behaviours, vocabulary, lifestyle, values, culture and customs—can influence our sanskars significantly. This is because we come into each other's vibrations as we go about our days. The sanskars thus created are a part of the third folder—environmental sanskars. It is easier to see physical influences like developing common interests with each other in a particular cuisine, clothing brand, TV show, music genre and so on. But our sanskars and personality also change subtly.

A child who begins schooling invariably picks up new words, ways of speaking and behaviours from there. Schooling provides the child a huge exposure beyond the circle of influence of family. This is what makes not just the choice of curriculum, extracurriculars and infrastructure, but the culture of the school extremely important. Besides imparting knowledge of the outer world, the classroom shapes the sanskars and personality of a child. They say education cannot be stolen from anyone, but so are sanskars. A sanskar, once created, becomes a part of the child's personality. There is no denying that studies are extremely important. But the grades, marks, prizes and awards alone should not become the sole goal of education.

Children often turn to friends rather than family for advice, support or enjoyment. Friends can influence their attitude, perception, thoughts, words, behaviours, habits and sanskars. Even if children do not necessarily create the same habit or sanskar which their friends might have, it is important to remember that the vibrations of close friends constantly influence their energy field. Negative sanskars in friends deplete a child's energy, while positive sanskars empower the child. This makes it imperative that children need to be advised to prioritize sanskars, when making friends and when developing their social circle. After all, they will start living in the strong circle of influence of the vibration of their friends for years. Soul consciousness reminds us to prioritize pure sanskars.

Sanskars created due to the environment could sometimes be so powerful that they can change or override the sanskars we had previously imbibed from our family. For instance, a child may have imbibed the sanskar of honesty from his parents. But as an adult, he may get influenced by colleagues to resort to unethical practices at the workplace. Consequently, he might stop using the sanskar of honesty and create a sanskar of manipulation. We really need to reflect on how deeply we can change because of the people we choose to be with.

Nowadays, media has emerged as perhaps the number one factor in shaping our environmental sanskars. It not just changes the sanskar of a few individuals, but impacts the entire society. Often, the content rendered by the media colours our opinions negatively about ourselves, other people and the world itself. It heightens the sanskars of anger, insecurity, fear and worry in society. Social media was intended to facilitate healthy communication and connections but today its misuse has increased unhealthy sanskars like comparison, jealousy, hatred and judgement. At times, even advertisements lead us to believe that buying more will earn us happiness and respect, although the truth is that happiness, which is emotional comfort, has nothing to do with material comfort. In Hindi, there is a saying that beautifully highlights the importance of our sanskars: 'Sanskar Se Sanskriti Se Sansar.' It means our sanskars (personality) create our sanskriti (culture), which in turn creates our sansar (our world).

Set 4: Sanskars Created through Your Willpower

What is that power that helps you achieve what you seek, despite hardships or distractions in life? Your willpower. By keeping your goals in mind, feeling inspired to achieve them, believing you can accomplish them and being determined to do what it takes, you invoke willpower. It supports you each time to take the required action. And the resulting sanskars are the fourth set: the sanskars created using willpower.

Using willpower means exercising our power to choose, to think, to be and to do what we want. Every time we use that inherent power within, it is our willpower in action. How is it that some people take just one week to stop an old sanskar of gossiping, while someone else just cannot resist small talk even after months of trying? Willpower is like a muscle that needs to be exercised. Most of us use it only in certain situations and not always. When we do not use it, we lose it. Each of us is gifted with the same amount of willpower. We can use this willpower to change any uncomfortable sanskar. But we believe that our sanskars cannot be changed. The fact is that we can change them at any moment. Willpower plays a crucial role in overriding any sanskar—regardless of whether we have carried them from past births, created them with our family's influence or formed them due to our present environment.

We have all used willpower to change our habits and sanskars at different points in our lives: the time we wake up, our diet, the content we consume, our body language, the words we use, behaviours we exhibit and so on. Once we have created a sanskar, it starts to run on auto mode. Our mind does not create two thoughts and our intellect does not need to take a decision. The sanskar comes into action automatically.

To change any habit, we need to first create thought options and then act. Let us understand with an example:

- Assume that you have been drinking coffee every morning for years. It means you drink coffee out of habit.
- One day, you read an article explaining that caffeine is not good for your health. You decide to switch to another beverage. Information enables you to create fresh thoughts and you start choosing another beverage.
- Your mind creates the options of herbal tea, lemon water and coconut water. Let us say the intellect decides that you drink coconut water.
- For a few days you will experience headache as a symptom of caffeine withdrawal. Your family also advises you to switch back to coffee. When you experiment with a new sanskar, be prepared to lose people's approval. But persisting through this transition period is important, for that is when your willpower is put to test.
- If you continue drinking coconut water for fifteen to twenty days, then it becomes a habit as natural as your earlier habit of drinking coffee. Thereafter, the mind does not create different thought options and the intellect will not need to take a decision. The two stages get bypassed.

Whether it is drinking coconut water, biting nails, binge-eating, being disorganized, seeking attention, cheating, complaining, gossiping, lamenting or anything else—this is exactly how all our habits and sanskars were created. And this is also how we can change any sanskar. Instead of focusing on the unhealthy sanskar and saying, 'I don't want to get angry', 'I don't want to get late' and so on, we simply need to focus on creating the new sanskars of peace and punctuality.

You might feel that shifting from coffee to coconut water is simple, but shifting from getting angry to being calm all the time is difficult. Yes, changing behavioural habits is easier than deep-rooted emotional sanskars. But the method remains the same. Behavioural habits of eating, drinking, exercising, sleeping or watching TV can be changed with one decision. Sanskars relating to emotions take conscious attention for a few days. The more we use our willpower to change behavioural habits, the easier it becomes to change our emotional sanskars.

How Willpower Gets Underutilized

Consider this example: Suppose a woman who is very irritable decides one morning: 'Today I will not get irritated. I will use patience in every situation'. However, in the next ten minutes, as she goes about her tasks, she tells herself, 'But ... it will be difficult for me ... I hope my housemaid does not repeat those silly mistakes. And my children ... they are so irritating ... and when my in-laws make noise while chewing breakfast ... I cannot stand that. Even last week I tried to be patient with all of them but I failed. Maybe irritation cannot vanish in one day ... it will take time. But today, I will really try hard...'

Notice how she creates one positive thought which is empowering, but soon follows it up with a train of negative thoughts which immediately disempowers her. With so many thoughts of self-doubt and deliberation, she has nearly lost sight of the goal. Her thoughts send a signal to the mind that success is a probability, which makes failure a possibility. The trick she missed is that once she decided to not be angry, she just had to create a single determined message: 'I am a powerful soul. I remain calm today. I use patience in every situation'. Her mind might interject every now and then with negative or wrong thoughts. But she once again needs to reiterate the same powerful thought. Her willpower fuels her motivation and self-belief to manifest her desire.

So let us constantly work on creating healthy sanskars. It does not matter even if we repeatedly failed in the past but now, using determination and attention, we can weaken any uncomfortable sanskar. It could be a gradual shift from the wrong to the right. But if we do not work on it, repeated use of the wrong sanskar strengthens it and depletes soul power. Never create the thoughts, 'I do not have willpower. I cannot do this. I always fail'. The mind and body will then accept these thoughts as reality.

Remind yourself daily: 'I am a powerful soul. I use my willpower to change any sanskar. Self-transformation is easy for me. Success is certain for me.' You will be well on the way to change any sanskar that you decide to change.

Set 5: Your Original Sanskars

Take a minute and answer these questions: why do you help a stranger cross the street? Why do you offer to help someone struggling to carry their grocery bags? Why do you say a silent prayer for an unknown person in an ambulance that passes by? Why do you offer food to a neighbour who is unwell? Why do you donate money, old books, clothes or furniture for charitable causes?

Many questions but they have a common answer: it is your original nature.

We have explored four sets of sanskars until now:

- Sanskars carried from our past lives
- Sanskars absorbed from our present family
- Sanskars developed due to our environmental influences
- Sanskars created using our willpower

Reflect on them again and you will realize that all these sanskars are what we create or acquire along our soul journey of multiple lifetimes. What sanskars did we carry when we, the souls, took our first bodily costume? The answer is: the fifth set of our sanskars, the original sanskars of every soul when it first begins its journey of birth and rebirth.

This journey is all about emerging, experiencing and radiating these seven original sanskars.

1. Purity
2. Peace

3. Love
4. Happiness
5. Power
6. Knowledge
7. Bliss

Each and every soul in this world, without an exception, has these seven sanskars present even at this moment. This means we are supposed to experience these sanskars constantly, naturally, effortlessly and automatically. We are also supposed to respond to every scene of life through these seven sanskars. We do experience them off and on. Some of us experience them and respond through these seven sanskars more often than others.

If purity, peace, love, happiness, power, knowledge and bliss are our original nature, then why are we experiencing lust, anger, greed, attachment, ego, hatred, jealousy, fear, guilt, regret and so on?

The Onset of Negativity

Suppose a workplace has four staff members who are in white uniforms. When they arrive for work in the morning, their clothes are clean and white. During the day, they play different roles and enter different environments. Someone has to deal with the soil while gardening, someone else has to work with coal for cooking, another has to repair cars in a garage and yet another spills food on his shirt while having lunch. This means their uniforms develop different stains of oil, grease, dust, sweat and food by the end of the day. The magnitude, colour and type of stains differ. But they all had started the day in white uniforms. When they know the original colour is white, they will ensure all their uniforms get washed and all the stains are removed.

In the same way, four people from a family start with their original nature of purity, peace, love, happiness, power, knowledge and bliss. But, over the soul journey of many lifetimes, living in different environments, families and situations, each of them creates stains—different acquired sanskars. One soul develops sanskars of hurt, jealousy and insecurity. Another soul develops sanskars of worry, anger and carelessness. The third soul may develop sanskars of hatred, domination and doubt. This means they all have different stains or acquired sanskars. All they need to do is remember that these are just stains developed over a period of time. Their original nature is the same.

This is true for all of us. We have all developed stains but originally, we are all pure souls. This understanding creates acceptance, empathy and respect for each other. It enables us to see each other as pure and peaceful souls. This is the truth and we need to remember this truth about ourselves and everyone else. Like the name suggests, our 'acquired' sanskars mean they are not 'original' and did not exist when we, as souls, took a body for the first time. Over our first few births we experience our seven original sanskars in action. That era is called heaven, paradise or Satyug, the Golden Age of the World. It is comparable to the first few hours of the morning when the uniform is spotlessly white.

As we continue the journey, our soul power gradually starts depleting. We start forgetting we are souls. This marks the beginning of the era of body consciousness, the era of ego, attachment and desires. We shift from soul-to-soul connections and start feeling attracted to the bodily costume. That is when the first traces of lust, anger, greed and fear are experienced. After a few more cycles of births and deaths, our soul power depletes further. We become increasingly body conscious and reach a point where we get completely disconnected from our original identity as souls. As a result, we start looking for our peace, love and happiness outside of us. We forget that they are within us. So, we reach the Iron Age of the World, called Kalyug, the era we are currently in. The time has now come for us not just to create a change but a paradigm shift—from complete body consciousness to a natural state of soul consciousness. This shift in us will create a paradigm shift in the world. Together, we will create the Golden Age, Satyug, once again, because when we change, our world changes.

Reinforcing Your Original Sanskars

Fundamentally, we have a vast database of sanskars at our disposal. We have the sanskar of peace but we also have the sanskar of aggression. We have the sanskar of happiness but we also have that of pain. It is up to us to keep using the right sanskars. The more they are used, the more powerful they become and before long, they will be our natural sanskars. Let us understand with an example:

- If a person uses anger more frequently, his sanskar of anger gets more and more reinforced. It goes into an automated mode. He often reacts angrily—scolding his children, disagreeing with colleagues, arguing with clients and so on.

- Even though he has the original sanskar of peace, it becomes dormant (submerged in his consciousness) and the sanskar of anger becomes dominant (emerges in his consciousness).
- When he gets angry so often, he believes anger is normal. It is not normal. It is just common.
- He feels he does not have peace of mind. He seeks to experience peace. So he goes on a holiday, watches the sunrise and sunset and meets friends.
- Suppose he realizes that peace is his nature and he just needs to use it, he starts to consciously respond with peace in every situation. He responds peacefully, say once, twice, thrice, ten times, twenty times—then the sanskar of peace becomes dominant. Anger becomes dormant.
- The sanskar of peace goes into an automated mode. He will 'naturally' respond peacefully thereafter.
- He creates a new belief: 'Peace is normal'.

We need to shift our belief from 'wanting' peace, love and happiness to 'being' peace, love and happiness.

Gently say these lines to yourself and feel every word while you say it:

I am a peaceful soul ... calm and easy in every situation ... I am a loving soul ... I understand people ... I accept them as they are ... my selfless love and kindness flows to all ... I am a happy soul ... scenes may go my way ... may not go my way ... the scene does not influence me ... I influence the scene ... I am a powerful soul ... I am the master of my mind ... The power to tolerate ... power to adjust comes natural to me ... I am a wise soul ... I choose my karma carefully ... I create a beautiful destiny ... I am a pure soul ... I expect nothing from people ... I only give ... I give love to all ... I give respect unconditionally ... I am a blissful soul ... I am untouched by what I do, what I achieve, what I use ... I am a divine soul.

Our objective is to play songs (sanskars) from the fifth folder so frequently that they play out in a loop. In other words, these original sanskars should be used so often that they become automatic. For example, each time we overcome a problem peacefully, we experience peace. It makes us comfortable and it increases soul power. The next time, being peaceful and stable becomes easier. We reach a stage where we can be calm in a crisis. Repeated use of the sanskars of peace, power, knowledge, happiness and love to face every circumstance of life strengthens them and simultaneously weakens our negative sanskars.

Soon, we will firmly believe, 'Peace, happiness, love and power are normal'. We will reach a stage where we constantly experience being happy, being love, being power and being divine.

10

Manifest the Life You Want

THERE ARE A FEW INTRINSIC, UNCHANGING AND powerful universal laws that govern our life. One of them is the Law of Attraction, which has gained momentum and created a buzz in the last few decades. People from all walks of life seem to be drawn to this law, to attract more happiness, health, good scores, a dream job, designation, steady income, new home and success. Given that we live in times of high uncertainty, who does not like to take advantage of this law to manifest all sorts of desires, from the mundane to the magnificent?

Being a spiritual law, the Law of Attraction has been codified in the Indian culture for centuries. People of the ancient times knew that this law touches the very foundation of our mind—our thoughts. They were clear that if they got their thoughts right, they would get their act right and thereby achieve the desired results. Besides, people had significantly higher soul power in those times than we have today. As a result, they easily created pure and powerful thoughts and attracted more peace, love and happiness into their lives. It was their natural way of living. But with time, like everything else, even soul power of human beings declined. So the need of the hour is for us to remain attuned with spiritual laws like the Law of Attraction, just as we do with scientific laws.

You Are a Vibrational Magnet

The phrases '*Sankalp se siddhi*', which means 'Our thoughts manifest', and '*Sankalp se srishti*' which means 'Our thoughts create our world', have been coined based on the principles of the Law of Attraction. Whatever our thoughts are focused on is what will manifest in our life. The energy we put out into the world comes back to us through what we attract. The way our life pans out is thus in our own control and we have the power to manifest whatever we want using the power of our thoughts. When we focus on a desired outcome, completely believe and sincerely act on it, our goal manifests. We will experience opportunities that align with our goals and desires, to manifest anything—whether it is love, wealth, freedom, relationships, travel, home, promotion and so on.

The crux of the Law of Attraction lies in the relationship between our thoughts and our destiny. It revolves around the most powerful tool of manifestation: our thought vibrations. Every thought is made up of energy and has a unique vibrational frequency. Vibrations are like radio signals that we constantly send to the universe. We need to tune our thought vibrations to a frequency adequate for achieving our goal or desire. We can take control of our thoughts, change our vibrations and manifest anything and everything we want. When we repeat a particular thought with conviction, we attract people, things and situations of the same frequency and draw them towards us. Positive thoughts attract positive situations and negative thoughts attract negative situations. So the more cognizant we are about the creation of positive thoughts in our mind, the better the position we put ourselves in to attract the reality we want. If we do not like what we are attracting, we simply need to change the thoughts we are sending out.

History reveals that we, as souls, lived in an era of complete purity and divinity. We simply had to create a determined thought and it would come true. Ascetics, yogis and saints had the power to manifest their thoughts or words instantly. When they were moved by compassion, they gave a blessing or a boon. When they were furious or wanted to ward off evil, they uttered a curse. All they had to do was to create a thought or state their wish verbally and it would manifest. Their blessings or curses could not even be reversed. So we were the people who had tremendous thought power a few births ago. Today, we are the same people who have declined to a state where we often struggle to think right.

Drifting far away from soul consciousness, we forgot our inherent qualities and instead got attracted to the dimension of body consciousness or ego. We started looking for peace in places, happiness in achievements, love from people and power in positions. Thus, we reached a stage where some of us used the Law of Attraction to attract external riches: to gain more wealth, to win over someone, to seal a business deal, to get a promotion, to buy an apartment and so on. Importantly, we did not take care of the self. Soul power was getting depleted: our mind was tired, the intellect was weak and sanskars were impure. In this state, we were using the law to fulfil our desires. The law seemed to work at times and failed at other times. We did not know why. Besides, there can never be a law for human greed to manifest. Harbouring endless desires is like drinking salt water. It only makes us thirst for more —a second home, the next promotion, greater recognition, a higher bank balance ...

Does the Law of Attraction Really Work?

The answer is yes—it works all the time. Whether or not we believe in it, understand it or are conscious of it, everything in our reality is a manifestation created by us through the Law of Attraction. At times, the outcome of this law even seems too good to be true. For that reason, there are critics and sceptics, as well as proponents of this law. Instead of asking, 'Do you believe in this law?', a better question would be, 'Do you understand how the law works in our lives?'

In fact, there are several daily life examples of the Law of Attraction working:

- You think about a person and they either call you or show up at your door.
- You hum a song in your mind and shortly afterwards, it starts playing on the radio.

- You have a question on your mind and someone gives an answer within minutes.
- You start thinking that a particular event will unfold and it does.

We feel intrigued since these are moments when we have no awareness of our vibration, energy or frequency. All we do is think of something and things happen. But when we understand the law, it becomes easier to crystallize our trust on its workings. Of course, we find several people who intentionally apply the law and create a reality of their choice.

We are all vibrational beings and so we are emitting energy all the time, even when we are sitting idle or sleeping. Our thoughts influence our actions and our actions influence our reality. So, in a way, **everything we have in life is a result of the Law of Attraction.** Whether we understand it or not, whether we accept it or not, this law is at work in our lives.

Choose to Attract Your Miracles

Look around and you will find people creating what they call miracles on a regular basis across the world.

- A professional visualizes landing his dream job continuously for months, to a point where he believes that he not only deserves it, but has already got it. He pictures himself entering the office, working at his desk, executing projects, attending meetings and so on. As he perseveres, he eventually manifests that desire.

- An athlete who loses a limb in an accident deeply desires to get back to running. He believes in his ability and works extremely hard. He does whatever it takes to build the required physical strength and mental toughness. He often visualizes participating and completing a running race. He feels the emotions and plays out the whole scene in his mind every day. In due course, he does participate in a race and cross the finish line.

We do not even have to look beyond our own selves. The quality of our thoughts—positive or negative—has determined the quality of our results. So it might be safe to assume all of us have ourselves practised the Law of Attraction and tasted small or big successes. When we got desired results, we termed it as a miracle, a blessing, a heaven-sent gift, magic, fortune or coincidence. And if we have been the kind of people who trusted something on one day but doubted it the next day, our contradicting vibrations did not yield results.

Pause for a moment and look around you. Everything that you see was once just a thought, whether it is a book, a table lamp, a cupboard, wall paint, a door, a computer or a phone. Every invention, discovery and innovation is a result of someone's thought. Our mind has created miracles in the outer world, a world that has several influences playing out at every moment. If the same mind focuses on the inner world, a world where there is no other influence, can we imagine its 'superpower' to make even the impossible possible?

A miracle is nothing but an outcome of channelizing the power of our thoughts to get what we desire. The human mind is so powerful that we can use it to overturn medical prognosis, astrological predictions, planetary influences, public opinions, lack of resources or any other unfavourable situation. When this happens, we call it a miracle. Look at some of the other miracles created by the human mind in the outer world. Someone who was expected to remain permanently bedridden is leading a normal life today. A person who could not afford three meals a day has turned into a millionaire today. Somebody who was once mocked for his acting skills, has won an Oscar award today.

If all these miracles are possible because of a powerful mind, think of the magic we can create internally: one who is aggressive today can become an embodiment of peace tomorrow. Someone who is fearful today can ooze confidence in the future. A person who believes in revenge can let go and forgive people. Somebody who is jealous can start cooperating and celebrate other people's success. An egoistic individual can become humble and modest.

Yet, why does this kind of inner transformation seem difficult or impossible? In fact, miracles in the inner world are easier to manifest than those in the outer world for the simple reason that the mind has to only focus on itself. Whether we consciously think right or not, the mind is going to create and radiate thoughts anyway. And it attracts the same energy back into our lives. So it is important that we remain masters of our mind and thereby become the masters of our lives. Let us leverage the Law of Attraction to create miracles in the inner world. Once we master this art, then manifesting miracles in the outer world becomes just a natural way of living.

But You Will NOT Attract What You Want ...

This title could be unsettling, given that we have already established the credibility of the Law of Attraction. We now know that it works all the time. The problem is that we are aware of the law, but most of us have not interpreted it correctly.

The Law of Attraction does not mean you get what you want. It actually means you get what you are.

Let us take an example. Suppose a mother desires a harmonious relationship with her young son, but is extremely possessive about him. Her control suffocates him and her dominance scares him. So she creates a thought, 'I want my son to bond well with me'. She keeps repeating that thought several times a day as per the Law of Attraction. She even visualizes it.

- What does she want? A close relationship with her child.
- Who is she? A controlling, possessive, critical and judgemental parent.
- Will her desire manifest? No, because of the gap between what she wants and who she is.

When she does not get the result, she doubts the law. And when she sees her son trying to avoid her, she gives up on the law, believing it does not work. When will her relationship with her son improve? When she remains calm and non-judgemental and accepts him and disciplines him with love. This means her vibrations need to have these energies for her desire to manifest. As a first step, she can use the Law of Attraction to change her sanskars. Thereafter, her relationship will automatically improve.

Suppose she creates the thoughts, 'I am calm. I accept my son as he is. We share a beautiful relationship'. When she thinks, believes and visualizes herself to be calm and accepting of her son, she radiates that energy. She practises calmness and acceptance. Gradually, her sanskars change. The vibration which she radiates to her son changes and his vibrations get influenced positively. Previously, she was radiating criticism and hence getting back rejection from him. Now, she radiates acceptance and hence receives acceptance. Their relationship starts shifting from conflict to harmony as her sanskars change.

It is important to internalize that the Law of Attraction works on the basis of vibrations: what we radiate is what we attract. Some of us wrongly believed that what we desire is what we radiate and attract. Each of us is a bundle of sanskars. And each sanskar, whether in thought or in action, is nothing but a vibration. Essentially, we are constant radiators of these vibrations.

When we intently practice the Law of Attraction, we hold a desire and create an affirmation for that desire. We coin the words of that affirmation carefully so that every time we think or say it, we radiate the right vibrations that match our desire. However, we are not radiators of only that one vibration alone. We radiate several other vibrations that we create as well, day after day and week after week. So, we need to be careful what we think, speak and do, especially if it is connected to our desire. Consider these examples:

- We want to manifest success in academics or at work. But what will be the result if we carry sanskars of laziness or procrastination?
- We want beautiful relationships. But throughout the day we are judging people, nagging, controlling or finding faults in someone or the other. Will our desire come true?
- We want to manifest good health. But we often eat junk food and rarely exercise. Will the Law of Attraction work?

In the above instances, the law does not give us results since our vibrations are not in sync with our desires. In fact, our vibrations are of the opposite quality. We persistently need to create sanskars that are at the frequency required for whatever it is we want to achieve. At times, we might have the required sanskars but we still do not get results. This is because we may not be creating focused intention. Intently practising the law enables us to achieve way more than what we set out to achieve. Let us be aware that the Law of Attraction cannot magically make something happen. The law is about focusing our intentions with determination to create or achieve more than our capacity at any given point in time. For these reasons, the Law of Attraction means you get what you are, not what you want.

Setting the Law in Motion

How many times do we voice these sentiments?

- *I am too lazy to exercise.*
- *I am not good enough. My success is doubtful.*

- *I lack determination.*
- *I am so scared. I wish I was brave.*

Reflect on this sentence: 'I am lazy.' Many of us tend to repeat it several times. Even people around us label us as lazy. It means from a Law of Attraction perspective, we are looking at laziness, thinking about laziness, talking about laziness, tuning into laziness, radiating laziness and attracting laziness. We barely realize that we are attracting the same energy that we want to repel. So, in this case, the right thought would be: 'I am hardworking'.

Let us do a simple exercise. Take a piece of paper and draw circles as per the instructions below. Draw each new circle as though you are tracing the previously drawn circles.

1. Draw a white circle.
2. Draw a black circle over it.
3. Draw two white circles, followed by four black circles.
4. Draw three white circles, followed by five more black circles.

What colour will the circle finally have? Black, as there are more black circles than white.

The same logic applies to our thoughts as well. We initially create pure and positive thoughts. But, thereafter, we forget and end up creating wrong and doubtful thoughts: 'I want to be an active person. But I am lazy. I should have completed this task by yesterday. I simply wasted time. I just don't feel like doing anything on most days. Lazing around is not right but I cannot change. This is how I am.'

Notice how each thought creates momentum for the next one. The negative vibration in every thought inevitably attracts more negativity back. The idea was to overcome laziness but the wrong thoughts intensify that very sanskar. If you create a thought four times a day but contradictory thoughts about the same topic fifteen times a day, then the thought which you created fifteen times will become the reality, since it is the predominant thought.

Exercising the Law

Whenever we hold a desire, there are two components which play out subsequently:

- Our desire: what we want in our reality
- Our vibrations: our beliefs, thoughts, words and actions

Let us consider a few examples to understand how to use the Law of Attraction to change uncomfortable sanskars.

Example 1: Suppose we have a sanskar of anger and we want to give it up. Our desire is to be peaceful. The present reality is that anger is still present in our life. But what happens to it in the future depends on the vibrations we create.

Desire: 'I want to be peaceful.'

The vibration needs to be: 'I am a peaceful being.'

But what happens throughout the day? We create other thoughts of doubt or despair: 'I am not able to give up anger ... it is difficult. One cannot get work done without using a little anger. Besides, people behave in strange ways—how else to discipline them if I do not shout at them? And what about kids? They trigger my anger. I have tried so many times ... I can't do it.'

This means our desire is to give up anger. But our vibration (thoughts) is that we cannot give it up.

Let us remember that our vibration becomes the reality and not our desire. So we need to instantly stop or cut wrong thoughts and replace them with the thought, 'I am a peaceful being'. Sometimes, we think, 'I am a peaceful being' once and then think, 'But I cannot give up my anger'. And then again, maybe twice we think, 'I am peaceful'. But later, we think a five more times, 'Nothing gets done without anger'.

Because of the dilution in our vibration, our desire does not match our vibration. The sanskar of anger therefore continues to come into action. When we create thoughts like 'I don't want to get angry' or 'I want to be free from anger', we are repeatedly using the word 'anger'. Repeated use of the word creates low vibrations. So it is important to state what we want to be rather than what we do not want to be.

Example 2: Often, when there is an argument or a quarrel, we say, 'Let us not talk about the problem but talk of the solution.' Suppose the present reality is that there is a conflict between the two of us. What happens next depends on the vibration we create.

Desire: To find a solution.

The vibration needs to be: 'What should be done next and how can it be achieved?'

But if we start dwelling on why the other person said or did something, we deviate from our desire to find a solution. Our curiosity leads only to blaming and criticizing. The other person may become defensive and turn the discussion into an argument. Every such thought takes us away from our desire of finding a solution and our vibrations of anger, judgement and blame will only intensify the problem.

Activating the Law with Affirmations

We need to create thoughts which match our desire. And we need to create a powerful thought about what we want, not just once but every single time. It is like planting a seed and nurturing it daily. This means once we create a thought, we will need to keep tuning into that vibrational frequency (or higher) until it manifests. Many people use reminders on their phone, post-it notes or other methods to help them sustain the same vibration. It enables them to remain aware of what they want and to how to think.

One of the most widely used methods to reinforce our beliefs about ourselves, our circumstances, other people or the world, is to use affirmations. How often do you find yourself creating such self-defeating, negative thoughts?

- *I shouldn't take up this course. I cannot work hard.*
- *I will surely fall ill. I have neither followed a healthy diet nor have got enough sleep.*

- *I do not deserve her friendship. She is better than me in every way.*
- *I give up. I cannot change my nature. This is who I am.*

Whether we realize it or not, we often repeat certain statements. The day we repeatedly create thoughts of failure, we experience failure. The day we repeatedly create thoughts of fear, our fear comes true. Why not apply the same principle and attract good things? This is what affirmations do.

Affirmations are a collection of consciously chosen sets of thoughts, stated either aloud or in our mind, intently and repeatedly with complete conviction. They enable us to remain focused on our desire or goal throughout the day, ensuring that our mind does not create vibrations of any other quality. Once the seed of optimism is planted in the mind, the resistance of fear or doubt is removed.

Self-affirmations are also like announcements we make about ourselves, about who we are and what we want. We do not use the vocabulary such as, 'I should', 'I want to', 'I wish', 'I will try', etc. We create thoughts beginning with 'I am …' as though we have already achieved what we want.

Let us revisit the four negative thoughts mentioned above. If we were to convert them into affirmations, they would be:

- *I am taking up this course. I am certain about working hard and succeeding.*
- *My body is healthy and will always be. I follow a proper diet and get the right amount of sleep.*

- *I value her friendship. I take inspiration and guidance from her to improve myself.*
- *I am determined to work on myself to transform into who I want to be.*

You might feel it is deceptive to state something that does not match the present reality.

No, it is not about deception. It corresponds to the law of '*Sankalp se siddhi*'. So do not look at what happens around you and create your thoughts. Create thoughts of what you want to see as your reality.

Affirmations provide the easiest way to embed pure and positive messages into the subconscious mind. These affirmations create an impression even when stated once. The impressions become deeper when the affirmations are repeated. So they go into the subconscious mind from the conscious and remain there, vibrating. Affirmations are like the white circles which we draw repeatedly to overwrite the black circles of negative thoughts of doubt, worry or fear. The mind believes that we have the potential to achieve our goal and, in the process, breaks boundaries of limiting self-beliefs. These vibrations radiate into the world and as we work towards our desires, the Law of Attraction responds, to manifest them.

When repeated over and over again, affirmations do not just remain as nice and positive thoughts but transform into our deep-seated beliefs. Affirmations hold the power of our convictions, the strength of our determination and the energy of our positive attitude. The language of affirmations eventually becomes a natural part of our thinking.

Visualization to Boost Success

The power of visualization is like a first line of defence against the negativity in our mind. Its power is to be experienced to be believed. As a simple tool to combine with affirmations, visualization has been a proven technique of mental rehearsal to foresee an ideal result or end goal in any situation. Visualization uses imagination, creativity and emotions to see and feel the affirmations. We create visuals of every affirmative statement or play out the scene on the screen of our mind. Then we hold on to that feeling and experience it as if it is the present reality.

Well begun is half done. Putting in as much detail as we can create—about our beliefs, thoughts, intent, feelings, awareness and the overall energy we invest repeatedly during visualization—gives us a good headstart to attracting what we want. The visualized image becomes clearer over time, with practice. The subconscious mind responds well to all these visual cues and therefore elevates the vibration of our desire further. Visualizing a positive future lets us remain unaffected by the negative influences of any failures in the past.

Students, athletes, artists and business leaders often use this power to enhance performance. Visualization has also been widely used as a complementary therapy in healing, where patients are taught to visualize the affected organ as receiving healing energy, overcoming the illness and functioning optimally.

Neuroscientists conducted an experiment in which a group of people used their five fingers to play piano notes two hours daily for five days. Another group had to only imagine playing those piano notes for five days. The brains of the volunteers were examined daily using the Transcranial Magnetic Stimulation (TMS) technique and there was little or no difference in the results between the two groups. This means our brain cannot tell the difference between the real and the imaginary. Visualization alters the workings of the brain and body.

Combining the Power of Affirmation and Visualization

Suppose tomorrow morning you decide: 'I will be calm, stable and happy the entire day today'.

However, you immediately follow it up with, 'But today I will meet that client who puts me off with his silly talk. He is so irritating. He has not made last month's payment. I hope not to lose my temper'.

All these thoughts are also affirmations. The power of doubts and apprehension negates the thoughts of happiness you had first created. So the odds of your being happy before, during and after meeting that client come down. Now, consider what happens when you consistently affirm and visualize: 'I am a happy being. I am calm and stable in every scene today. I accept people. I radiate happiness'.

Visualize how the meeting goes. You are calm as you speak powerful words to the client. You listen to his opinion which differs from yours but you understand his perspective. Thereafter, you politely assert that he needs to clear his dues. He agrees, pays the dues and apologizes for the delay. There is an energy of harmony throughout the meeting.

Your mind gets programmed about how you will BE in whatever you DO. The affirmations override your old, limiting belief that happiness depends on people and on circumstances. The visualization of remaining internally peaceful at home, while travelling, at the workplace or at a social gathering, will take you closer to manifesting it. So you start the day with affirmations and visualization. Thereafter you do not create irritation and apprehension in the morning about the meeting. Instead the day begins on a positive note and you look forward to the meeting. During the day you pause a couple of times and repeat the affirmations. It is important to remember that while you are creating those affirmations, your vibrations are reaching your client. Therefore, he also starts feeling positive about meeting you. He starts creating thoughts about clearing the dues.

Repeated affirmations keep you calm and enable you to respond in the right way to the events of the day and in all your interactions. Each time you respond well, you increase your inner strength and deepen your sanskar of peace. You radiate positive vibrations to your body and make it healthier. You radiate an energy of calmness to the people you think of. And you radiate peace into the environment, influencing others around you.

With all this, your affirmations would have become your state of being, by the time you enter the meeting with that client. You firmly believe that the meeting will be a great experience for both of you. When such strong conviction and positive vibrations radiate from you and reach your client repeatedly throughout the day, the meeting turns out to be better than what you visualized.

Even if the client does not return the complete amount or is unable to pay you this time, your vibrations of calmness and acceptance will create a positive experience for him. It influences him to try his best and settle the accounts soon.

Creating high vibrational thoughts and manifesting a desired result involves these simple steps:

1. Affirm what you want with conviction.
2. Visualize the scene in as much detail as you can.
3. Feel every emotion.
4. Repeat the above steps often.
5. Take actions that align with your thoughts.
6. See your desire manifesting.

Let us also understand how the day would have unfolded, had you not affirmed and visualized a favourable outcome. Minutes after you wake up, you think about meeting the client. The thought triggers a host of past memories and you feel annoyed. By the time you have breakfast, you would have created several negative thoughts and apprehensions. You suspect that he will find excuses to not pay you today. Your vibrations of anger, irritation and anxiety reach the client. He also feels uncomfortable about the meeting because your negative energy has started influencing him. He thinks of ways to avoid paying you the amount, because your vibrations have radiated to him.

Can you see that these negative and wrong thoughts you create are also affirmations and visualizations? And can you see how they too will manifest? Predictably enough, your fears come true during the meeting: your conversation is not pleasant and he refuses to the pay the dues. That is when you are likely to say to him, 'I knew you will not give me my money even today. I was sure you will come up with excuses and turn this meeting into another bitter experience. And that is exactly what has happened.' The fact is, it is not that you knew what would happen. It is simply your wrong thoughts manifesting themselves because you repeated them many times with conviction.

Ten Life-changing Daily Affirmations

By now, we know that affirmations can be created for every situation and every occasion. But it helps to have a basic set handy so that we can practice them routinely without having to wonder what to think. Revisiting them every day implies we radiate our desire to the universe consistently, so the Law of Attraction gets invoked each time we send out these vibrations. In that context, listed here are ten basic affirmative statements that you can take note of to see a marked improvement in different and important areas of your life:

1. *I am a powerful soul ... calm and stable always.*
2. *I am a happy soul ... easy and relaxed always.*
3. *I am fearless ... I am confident.*
4. *I am a giver ... I give love, I give respect to everyone, always.*
5. *I forgive everyone ... I release the past ... I live in the present.*

6. *I accept everyone ... everyone accepts me ... I have beautiful relationships.*
7. *My mind and body are perfect and healthy ... and will always be.*
8. *I excel at everything I do ... success is certain for me ... abundance is my reality.*
9. *God's powers and blessings are a circle of divine light around me ... my protection shield.*
10. *My life is perfect and will always be.*

The Art of Creating Affirmations

Affirmation is a language. Even children as young as five years old can be taught to use affirmations. While they learn their mother tongue and other languages, they should be taught the language of affirmations as well. It then becomes the language in which they think. We can all easily create our own affirmations—for health, relationships, career or any other situation.

The law can be written as a simple equation:
Thought = Reality

Affirmations have a construct that we already have/are what we want. Create the thought that exactly matches the reality you want. Carefully observe the difference in the language of affirmation and hence in the reality in these two sentences:

- If you create an affirmation, 'I want peace', the reality will be that you will keep wanting peace.
- If you create an affirmation, 'I am peace', the reality will be that you experience peace.

Along similar lines, let us never say 'I want to be healthy.' The affirmation should be, 'My mind and body are healthy and will always be.'

In addition to the basic set of affirmations, like the ten sample affirmations explained previously, you may add a few more (not too many) depending on any important event like exams, a business deal, surgery, financial challenge and so on. But remember to keep the basic set unchanged. Use these guidelines to create a basic set of affirmations:

Step 1: Think about the areas of life where you want to have or experience something. Create short, powerful and positive statements about them. Write the affirmations in the 'now', as though you are already experiencing what you desire in the present.

Step 2: Most self-affirmations are 'I am' statements. Some examples are:

- *I am a happy soul.*
- *I am a powerful being.*
- *I am always confident.*
- *Success is certain for me.*
- *I am healed.*
- *I am at ease, I have more time than I need.*

Ensure they do not contain low vibration words as they get repeated several times and hence are like the code that reformats the mind. Refrain from using phrases such as 'should not', 'should be', 'I want', 'I wish', 'will become', 'will try' or 'hope to'.

Step 3: Affirmations teach your mind the normal way of thinking. Hence, it is important to leave out what you want to eliminate or avoid. Notice how low-vibration words are eliminated in these examples.

Instead of this ...	Use this ...
I no longer get angry.	I am always peaceful.
I am not lazy.	I am hardworking.
I overcome fears.	I am confident.
I have stopped eating junk food.	I eat healthy food.
I will not be late to work.	I reach office before time.

Step 4: Often adding a few more words can add value to the affirmation, make it more comprehensive and distinct. At other times, the choice of a better word can uplift the affirmation instantly. So look to add a few details or use higher-vibration words wherever you can.

Instead of this ...	Use this ...
I am happy.	I am always happy, under all circumstances.
I am peaceful.	I use peace in every interaction with everyone.

Instead of this ...	Use this ...
I am healthy.	*I am perfectly healthy and will always be.*
My relationships are smooth.	*My relationships are beautiful and harmonious.*
I have enough money.	*I have more money than I need.*

Step 5: At times, the situations could be challenging or our unhealthy sanskars could be deep and difficult to uproot. Changing them becomes easier when we use more than just one line of affirmation. Here are a few examples:

- To change a sanskar of anger: 'I am a peaceful soul. I accept everyone as they are. I express my opinion but with dignity. I get work done with discipline. Peace and patience are my nature.'
- To change a sanskar of being late: 'I am a powerful soul. I can be everything I choose to be. I am always punctual and I always reach before time.'
- To improve physical health: 'I am happy soul. My body is perfect and healthy, and will always be. Every organ is functioning optimally. All my health parameters are well within the normal range.'
- To heal from a specific illness: 'I am a powerful soul. (If any parameter is not normal) My cholesterol levels are normal ___ (specific value/figure). (For any blockage, clot, or tumour) ___ has dissolved, disappeared. My ___

(organ name) is perfect healthy. My body is perfect and healthy.'

- To harmonize a relationship: 'I am a loveful soul. My relationship with ___ (person) is a perfect relationship. I have released all past emotions. I radiate love and acceptance. My relationship is strong and will always be.'
- To achieve academic success: 'I am a knowledgeable soul. I am sincere. I am focused. My concentration power is at the highest. I perform more than my capacity. I have achieved ___ (marks or grade). My success is guaranteed.'

Making Affirmations Work for You

Once you have the affirmations, you are ready to practise them. It would be nice if you can visualize the entire scene with as many details as possible—the place, goal, sounds, objects, colours, person, interaction and so on. Doing all this makes it easier for your subconscious mind to believe more deeply. And what you believe will be what you achieve or attract.

Even if you are not always able to visualize or say your affirmation with feelings, simply do one thing: state the affirmations. Even if you do not feel them, even if you do not believe them, just keep stating them daily.

While there are no rigid rules about the time or frequency to state or revise affirmations along with visualization, there are a few guidelines for optimizing their power and effectiveness:

1. There are two specific time windows in a day when your subconscious mind is the most active: immediately after

waking up in the morning and just prior to sleep at night. Take advantage of these times. Start your day by stating the affirmations every morning upon waking up. Say them slowly and with conviction, visualizing each statement. Repeat at least three times to internalize every thought and embed it into your subconscious mind. The affirmations then go into the deeper layers of your mind. It is like planting a seed deep inside the soil and not just leaving it on the surface.

2. Repeat the affirmations every night, again visualizing them. It is a good practice to write them slowly and neatly in a diary that can be kept by your bedside. Let them be the last thoughts on your mind as you go off to sleep. They will get embedded into your subconscious and radiate to your body and into the environment for the next six hours.

3. During the day, if you start creating doubts or concerns or any other form of negative thought relating to your affirmations, immediately stop and repeat the affirmations.

4. Most of us are taught to connect to the divine and offer gratitude before having a meal. There is yet another reason for this. Food absorbs vibrations from the surroundings, so it is important to create high-energy words around them. Take a ten-second pause and state your affirmations (you may even shorten them) before consuming food and water. Very soon, it develops into a habit, as natural as washing your hands before a meal.

Water absorbs the state of mind of the people in its vicinity. If they experience anger, pain or stress, then water traps these vibrations. When you drink such water, vibrations in the water will start influencing your thoughts. '*Jaisa pani, waisi vani*' is a popular line in Hindi, which means as is the water we drink, so will the words we speak. It is your thoughts which will come into words and actions. Therefore, energize water by stating affirmations before you drink it.

The goal is to affirm and visualize your desires at least eight to ten times a day. Within a month, you will start believing them and feeling them, and in a couple of months, you will start seeing results. It is important to not keep changing your affirmations frequently. Revise the same set every day to make them more effective.

The Law of Attraction is not magic per se but it surely can work like magic when you practise it intently and systematically. Apply it in every aspect of life and make the creation of miracles a normal way of living.

11

Seven Practices for Self-care

Y OU DECIDE TO GO ON A LONG ROAD TRIP TO DISCOVER
and explore places you have never been to. Will you
randomly pack things and hit the road? Not at all. You will
plan every aspect—the itinerary, who your fellow travellers
will be, the route, the condition of your car, food, clothes,
health and safety gear, camping supplies, entertainment
kit, toolkit, license, insurance documents and so on. Your
meticulous preparation and a good attitude will make the
journey enjoyable and worthwhile.

Self-transformation is a similar journey. Taking you
inward, it lets you discover and explore aspects about yourself,
some of which you might not have been aware. All you need is
to plan and prepare the resources needed for this endeavour:
your mind, body, time and energy.

You are now able to say, 'This is who I want to be, this is what I want to do and this is what I want to give to the world.' You are self-aware and taking personal responsibility for how you think and feel. You are making significant progress in connecting with your innate nature and rising to your inner potential. You certainly want all these powerfully positive changes to seep into every aspect of life.

Ask yourself: 'How can I use my inner resources on this journey of achieving emotional independence, sanskar transformation and soul consciousness?'

The Seven Key Practices

In airplanes, you might have noticed the instructions written on oxygen compartments above every seat: 'In case of an emergency, secure your own mask before helping others.' Visualize yourself on the middle seat, with your parent and your child on either side. Suppose there is air turbulence and the oxygen masks drop down. Will you be able to put a mask on yourself first, instead of helping them? However difficult or selfish it might seem, your family's safety lies in you doing so. Thereafter you will not run out of oxygen and can help them to get their masks on. This is the principle of care and protection: take care of yourself so you can offer better care to others. Unfortunately many people equate self-care with being selfish or self-indulgent. That is so not true.

The goals of emotional independence, self-awareness and self-mastery need us to practise self-care. We are experts at setting such goals, but often our routines do not support these goals since they leave self-care out of the plan. When we do not get the desired results, we tend to abandon our goals sooner or later. Fortunately, we are creatures of habit, so self-care can happen by creating these seven incredibly simple and easy habits:

1. **Habit # 1:** Make a winning start to the day
2. **Habit # 2:** Boost your emotional and physical immunity
3. **Habit # 3:** Recharge after every hour
4. **Habit # 4:** Go on an information diet
5. **Habit # 5:** Keep every karma right
6. **Habit # 6:** Change your destiny with every meal
7. **Habit # 7:** Ease into a deep and restful sleep

Practising them might not make your problems disappear. Life will continue to be a combination of the mediocre and the magical, of the good and the not-so-good events. But you will no longer be the same person. You will develop enough resilience through these habits, resolve problems and do whatever it takes to reach your goals.

Habit # 1: Make a Winning Start

Reflect on these questions:

- How do you typically feel when you open your eyes every morning: fresh or groggy?
- At what time do you wake up on weekdays? What about weekends and holidays?
- Do you get off the bed immediately upon waking and go about your chores?

If you are ready with your answers, compare them with these common statements:

- *I love a new day. It is the first day of a new life that I can create.*
- *I am not a morning person. I wake up at 8 a.m. and rush through my chores.*
- *My day has to begin with the phone, newspaper and coffee.*
- *I hate getting out of bed. It is a real struggle every morning.*

Each new day that rolls by gives us the most valuable resource: the gift of time. This gift is a precursor to another precious gift: our thoughts. And there we are, at the crack of dawn, ready to use every moment and every thought to move closer to our self-transformation goals. So, the first of the seven habits ought to be about easing into a new day. This habit is best complemented with three small actions: rising early, giving gratitude and affirming our desires.

1: Rise Early

Charting out a plan? Want new ideas? Need to learn something? Seeking clarity? Looking for a solution? Ask anyone how to get these done and they are likely to suggest, 'Wake up early in the morning and work on them'. Perhaps you have also experienced breakthrough solutions out of the blue in the early morning hours.

For centuries, *Amrit Vela*, also known as *Brahma Muhurat*, has been widely regarded as an ideal time to wake up. 'Amrit' means nectar and 'Vela' means time or moment in Hindi. It is an auspicious and powerful time window that offers the possibility to become like the Brahman or the Creator, so it is ideal to seize that time and work on becoming who we want to be. This predawn time window is approximately between 3:30 a.m. and 5:30 a.m., when the atmosphere is filled with divine energy.

If you want to drive to another city, you perhaps choose to do this early in the morning because of minimal traffic and for a comfortable driving experience. If you need to download large files from the internet, you prefer early mornings to take advantage of the fast internet speed and no network congestion. Likewise, if you want to tap into the riches of your inner world, activate your intuition and connect to the divine, Amrit Vela is most conducive since there is minimal traffic of thoughts in our mind and in the environment. Otherwise, meditating or sitting in silence takes comparatively more time and effort as the day progresses.

Compare the vibration of your office with that of a meditation or prayer room. It is like the difference between vibrations at 4 a.m. (Amrit Vela) and 8 a.m. The meditation room has peaceful and powerful vibrations because your mind does not create lower-vibration thoughts there. Besides, pure thoughts imply fewer thoughts. The deep silence inside a room is an energizer. Nearly everyone around us is in a state of sleep at Amrit Vela, so not just external noise but the internal noise of human minds is negligible at that time. There are very few thoughts and almost no palpable words or behaviours at that time. Negative vibrations are minimal and pure vibrations are high. So, the mind and intellect are more receptive to learning, grasping, analysing and absorbing new information. People wake up to meditate, pray, introspect and reflect during Amrit Vela. Even places of worship engage in prayers, chants and other forms of spiritual endeavours involving high vibrations that energize the environment at this time. Take a moment to close your eyes to visualize the atmosphere at Amrit Vela and tomorrow, take the next step of waking up at that time and feel the powerful energy.

Shifting your wake-up time might cause a few days of inconvenience to reset the body's internal clock, but the advantages far outweigh the troubles. It is recommended to rise at least by 5 a.m., if you cannot wake up earlier due to medical reasons or any other unavoidable circumstances. The adage 'Early to bed and early to rise makes a man healthy, wealthy and wise' sums up the benefits. Of course, it means you need to go to bed early. We will learn about a healthy sleep routine shortly.

2: Welcome the Day with Gratitude

Immediately upon waking up, do you reach for your phone or newspaper or the TV remote? The information you feed your mind in the morning lays a foundation for the quality of thoughts you create through the day. If you absorb messages of the world around you, your emotions will be what the world is like today. You will be more likely to react impulsively to situations. So refrain from checking work emails, messages and social media, engaging in phone conversations, reading the newspaper or watching TV for at least one hour upon waking. All these activities can wait, unless there is an emergency, and we know emergencies come up rarely.

As soon as you wake up, sit upright on your bed for five minutes, alert and awake. With your first few thoughts, give gratitude. We are all in a continuous interplay of karmic accounts with people, nature and the objects we possess. When we offer gratitude to them all for their roles and purposes in our life, our attitude influences how we think, feel and treat them. Gratitude creates a feeling of abundance, of being blessed, being cared for and being comfortable. It is not about what we have or how much we have. Gratitude is an attitude to develop even if nothing is going right in life. Make it a daily practice to be grateful to:

- **God**: For the life you are blessed with.
- **Your mind and body**: For being healthy and serving you. They help you to connect, express and experience life at every moment.
- **People**: For their roles, love and care. Be grateful even to people who have been difficult since they have enabled you to become emotionally stronger.
- **Nature**: For nurturing and sustaining you. For instance, every day, we do not acknowledge water flowing from a tap. But on the day a tap goes dry, we complain endlessly.
- **Time**: For cooperating with you to get things done when you want.
- **Objects you possess**: For giving you comfort, convenience and utility.

When you shift to a higher frequency of gratitude, you gradually end the tendency of complaining or criticizing. You experience higher acceptance and respect for what you have.

3: Revise Your Affirmations

You do not even need to get off your bed to practise this. Just stay alert, state and visualize your affirmations, as explained in the previous chapter. Repeat them at least twice or thrice to internalize the thoughts and embed them into your subconscious mind.

Habit # 2: Boost Your Emotional and Physical Immunity

Regardless of how challenging the previous day was, the beauty of a new day is that our issues are several hours behind us. Every morning, our first responsibility is to energize the soul so that we can experience and sustain peace, patience, acceptance and forgiveness. Energizing happens with meditation, spiritual study and exercising. Just as we till a field before planting seeds, we need to prepare the self, taking out thirty minutes for the mind and thirty minutes for the body, and then we can face the day with the right energies.

1: Practise Meditation

Meditation is derived from the word 'mederi' which means 'to heal'. What does it heal? It heals the soul, which in turn heals the body, our relationships, career, nature, life and the world itself. As far as possible, meditate at the same time every day. Avoid sitting on the bed for meditation as it has vibrations of sleep. Today, homes are planned to have separate rooms for gaming, music, gym and even laundry. The most important space every house must have is a room exclusively for meditation. If having an entire room is not possible, choose a quiet corner within a room and cordon off that area with a partition. Ensure the space for meditation is not close to TV or any other distraction. The balcony or terrace may also be used.

Until you learn meditation, use a guided meditation commentary. Playing soft music creates a soothing effect on your mind. Sit upright in a comfortable posture and remain alert. It is ideal to sit cross-legged but you may also sit on a chair. Practise keeping your eyes open during meditation so that you will gradually reach a meditative state even while doing other activities. Besides, keeping the eyes closed might induce sleep. Remember that the objective of meditation is not to stop thinking, although many people try doing it and give up. They become unsuccessful since the human mind cannot stop thinking. Meditation is also not about allowing all sorts of thoughts to simply flow for thirty minutes or so. It is about channelizing your thoughts in the direction you want to take them. Meditation involves all the three faculties of the soul: thought creation, visualization and experience. The experience recorded on the soul as an impression starts changing your sanskar.

The first stage is to stabilize yourself in soul consciousness. Create a thought of being a pure, peaceful, powerful soul (you may consider any of the seven original soul qualities). Visualize yourself as a point of light shining at the centre of your forehead. Hold that thought for as long as you can. Your feeling of peace and purity will get recorded on the soul. Initially, other intruding thoughts might occur. Without entertaining them or getting entangled in them, gently guide your mind back.

The second stage is to connect to the Divine. Like each of us is a soul or energy, the Divine or God is also energy. He is the 'Supreme' Soul. The word Supreme does not mean God is bigger in size. It means God is supreme in qualities and powers, thus being the ocean of peace, love, bliss, purity, wisdom, happiness and power. Visualize His powers to be like the sunrays falling on you, filling and energizing you. His divine energy vibrations heal the soul. You can then radiate this energy to your body also to heal it. You may even visualize another soul on the screen of your mind and radiate God's vibrations to that soul. The vibration will heal that soul and also transform your karmic relationship with that person. During meditation you may also share your thoughts or questions with the Divine and create a personal relationship with God.

Sit back, relax and go through a meditation experience with this guided commentary. As you read each thought, visualize it and start feeling it. You may record it and use the recording for a few days. After a few days, you would not need it as you will become capable of creating meditative thoughts on your own.

I relax my body … I visualize myself as a tiny point of light … a little star … shining in the centre of the forehead … this is 'I' … I, the being of light … I am a soul … I am the master of my body … I am the master of my mind … I am the creator of my thoughts … feelings … words … and behaviours … I am a pure soul … I am connected to God … the Supreme Power … the ocean of virtues and powers … I connect to God's vibrations of purity … peace … love

... wisdom ... I absorb them fully ... I experience these qualities within me ... I emerge them in every karma ... I vibrate at a frequency of divinity ... God's powers and blessings are my protection shield ... I am encircled by God's blessings ... I am pure ... I am powerful ... I play my roles with humility ... my selfless love and kindness flows to all ... I expect nothing from people ... I am a giver ... I give love to all ... I give respect unconditionally ... I am a peaceful soul ... I accept every situation ... I accept every person's behaviour ... I radiate love, respect and care to every soul ... I am a powerful soul ... The power to tolerate ... power to adjust, come naturally to me ... I am a wise soul ... I choose ... I affirm ... I visualize ... my vibrations heal my body ... my vibrations change situations .... my vibrations transform people ... my vibrations attract success ... I manifest what I choose .... I create my destiny of happiness, health, harmony.

2: Nourish Your Mind with a Pure Information Diet

Pure, powerful and positive information is a rich emotional diet for the mind, which builds emotional immunity. Consume content that is rich in compassion, acceptance, respect, unity, patience, happiness and forgiveness. You may choose from spiritual texts, self-transformation books or videos, or messages from discourses. In your own words, summarize or mark out one or two important points in a precise manner. Revise the points and look to apply the wisdom practically during the day. For instance, you may read, 'Forgive people and let go.' As the day goes by, you may find someone being wrong to you or making a mistake. That would be the time to practise what you read: forgive and let go.

You might have experienced that sometimes the content you come across is life-changing or it is exactly what you needed to hear. Even if it is unrelated to an ongoing issue in your life, healthy content certainly empowers your mind to face challenges. Systematic daily study keeps you in an orbit of positivity, helps you to remain in the learning zone and increases resilience.

3: Activate Your Body with a Workout

Keep aside at least thirty minutes to walk, jog, exercise, practise yoga or swim. Enjoy the activity to increase its effectiveness. If you cannot do it in silence, ensure that you watch or listen to pure and positive content. This way, you can double the benefits by empowering the mind while energizing the body. Do not allow the mind to drift into thinking about challenges, other people, the past, the future or indulge in gossip. Otherwise, the body gets physically energized but wrong thoughts or conversations radiate disempowering vibrations. Breathing exercises can be done along with conscious creation of right thoughts, since an emotionally fit mind radiates healing energy to the body. For instance, visualize yourself inhaling strengths and exhaling emotional toxins with thoughts such as:

Inhale: *I am a peaceful, powerful soul.*
Exhale: *I throw out irritation and anger.*

Inhale: *I am a loving soul, I respect everyone.*
Exhale: *I release the toxins of past hurt.*

Habit # 3: Recharge after Every Hour

Our mind is pulled and pushed in a thousand directions throughout the day. So it is capable of derailing us from calmness and leaving us in chaos. It can also get affected by the vibrations radiating from our surroundings. If someone around us is stressed, our own sanskar of stress can get triggered. If somebody is gossiping, we might feel tempted to participate. This effectively means that all our early morning efforts of energizing the mind and body could go for a waste within hours—at the breakfast table over an argument at home, at a traffic signal or during the first hour at the workplace. And we will be left with a depleted and disturbed mind for the rest of the day.

Imagine the plight of roads if there were no traffic controlling mechanisms in place. There would be chaos and accidents. The same holds true for the traffic of thoughts in our mind. Thoughts need to be monitored and regulated to avoid emotional chaos. This simple mechanism is called the Traffic Control of the Mind, where after every one hour, we pause and meditate for one minute to energize the mind and carry that energy into the next fifty nine minutes. We can choose any of the seven original soul qualities and meditate on it just for 60 seconds to bring that quality in action. Here is a sample you can use:

Peace

I am a peaceful soul ... Irrespective of whatever the situation may be ... I remain calm, easy and peaceful ... I always choose peace ... I am stable in every situation ... with every kind of behaviour.

Love

I am a loving soul ... Different people, different nature ... I understand them ... I accept them as they are ... I am compassionate ... I feel right ... I behave right ... always.

Purity

I am a pure soul ... I need nothing from people ... I am a giver ... I am selfless ... Everything I watch, read, listen, eat or drink is pure ... Humility is my personality.

Happiness

I am a happy soul ... I give my best in every instance ... my happiness is untouched by the outcome ... I achieve my goals with happiness ... I am content always.

Wisdom

I am a wise soul ... I choose my karma carefully ... I decide my future ... every incident in my life is right ... it is beneficial for me ... I create a beautiful destiny.

Power

I am a powerful soul ... I am the master of my mind ... I am the master of my sense organs ... I am the master of my life ... I can do anything I choose to do.

You may wonder if one minute makes a difference. It certainly does. Usually, we move from one task to the next, carrying the emotional baggage of the previous activity.

Following the traffic control mechanism for the mind prevents emotional clutter. Just as we prepare our body to carry out different activities, we need an inner preparation of the mind. After all, it is the mind which is going to get every task done. So even if you are in the middle of a conversation or watching TV or cooking, take a pause, recharge and then return to what you were doing. It is particularly beneficial to pause for a minute and regulate thoughts before embarking on important tasks. Here are a few examples:

- **Studies**: *I am a powerful soul. My memory and concentration power are at the highest. I perform more than my capacity. Success is certain for me.*
- **Cooking**: *I am a peaceful soul. I cook with love and care. Every morsel is filled with God's blessings. This food nourishes everyone with health and happiness.*
- **Meeting**: *I am a pure soul. Each of us carries pure intentions for the task. I talk to them respectfully. I listen to them. They listen to me. The meeting is a pleasant experience.*
- **Office Work**: *I am a wise soul. I am sincere and ethical. I complete every task accurately before time. I come out of my comfort zones. I am my best version in every task.*

Habit # 4: Go on an Information Diet

Just as food nourishes the body, information nourishes the soul. We have already established how every piece of information or content we consume becomes a source for the mind to create thoughts. Our thoughts decide our destiny, so essentially, we become what we read, watch, listen and speak.

Another common source of negative information comes from conversations that revolve around the things we can do nothing about—like someone else's weaknesses, problems or mistakes. Yet we often lend an attentive ear. When someone gives an opinion about a person, it is their perspective based on their sanskars. How does someone with a sanskar of criticism, jealousy or worry, talk about others? This means the first layer of the wrong emotional diet fed to us is about the weakness of the person being talked about. The second layer is of the weakness of the person talking to us. We add the third layer of our own weakness by listening to it. Thus, we end up consuming three layers of a toxic emotional diet in a matter of minutes. This is an unnecessary baggage to carry despite wanting to remain light and happy.

By discussing someone, they do not change. You change because you have consumed negative information. To stay away from a toxic emotional diet, you have four options.

Option 1: You refuse certain dishes, regardless of how tempting they are or how lovingly they are offered. Extend this discipline to refuse unhealthy information. Decline politely but assertively, stating that you do not want to listen about anyone else's issues, sanskars or behaviour.

Option 2: Shift the conversation from being problem-oriented to solution-oriented. Shift the focus on how the person talking to us could handle the situation. You are then discussing about sanskars of the person talking to you, rather than the sanskars of the person who is not present.

Option 3: Help the person talking to you to see the perspective of whoever they gossip about. You can also urge the person to focus on virtues rather than weaknesses.

Option 4: Refuse to passively listen to what is being said, in the name of courtesy, obligation or fear. Otherwise, it amounts to you endorsing their views.

Habit # 5: Keep Every Karma Right

The high vibrations accumulated with the first four habits can be channelized in a worthwhile way. Let their result reflect in your every thought, word and action. After all, you do not want to engage in wrong karmas during the day. Otherwise, the very purpose of soul strengthening gets defeated. Karma includes your every thought, word, action and behaviour. Make every karma a blessing for yourself, other people and situations. You have already started focusing on right thinking. Now, you can also work on elevating your words and behaviour.

Taking care of your words is a big step in keeping your karmas right. Your vocabulary reflects your beliefs and perceptions about yourself, another person or a situation.

When you see wrong sanskars or problems with yourself, family, friends, colleagues or even strangers, you perhaps feel upset. Repeated thinking and talking of the reality radiate vibrations which strengthen the wrong sanskars and escalate problems. Consciously create only pure, powerful, positive words in daily communication so that you gradually shift to a vocabulary of affirmations, which translate to a vocabulary of blessings.

Shift Your Vocabulary from This …	To This …
Not sure if I can complete this task.	*I am certain about completing this task.*
This challenge might overwhelm you.	*You will cross this challenge easily.*
My children fall ill frequently.	*My children are always fit and healthy.*
The world is full of misery and pain.	*The world is full of beauty and wonder.*
I don't think they can afford a car.	*I am sure they will buy a car of their choice.*

Feel the words in the second column and sense the energy shift as you read them. Notice how every word creates power and happiness in your mind, radiates healing energy to your body, empowers people around you and uplifts your surroundings. Other people may or may not understand your words but your vibrations reach them and empower them to change their situations.

Karma comprises of your actions and behaviours, so strive to keep them pure. Here are a few simple ways to do so:

- Drop the emotional baggage of pain, fear or resentment you are holding onto. Refrain from arguments and conflicts. Forgive people, understanding that what they did in the past was due to their nature, their perspective, their mood that day or it was a consequence of your past karmic account which is now settled.

- Check for any subtle or physical addictions, either to experience happiness, to feel energized or to distract your mind. Use spiritual knowledge and meditation to heal emotional blockages, increase willpower and reinforce that happiness is your original quality. You will no longer need anything externally to create feelings of happiness inside.

- Refrain from comparison, competition and peer pressure. Use your values and principles even if no one else is using them. Your life is your journey to your destination at your speed, using your capacity, based on your values and principles.

Check the quality of your karmas when earning money. This money gets used right from fulfilling your basic needs to making your life comfortable. But the money you earn is not just visible currency. It also carries the invisible energy of the way you earned it, which includes your intentions, thoughts, beliefs, behaviour, principles and ethics. Essentially, everything you buy with money—food, clothes, property, jewellery, furniture and so on—has the vibration of your energy. Money earned using the highest ethics vibrates with purity and positivity. When you earn in this way, you not only bring home material wealth but also blessings and the energies of peace, happiness and love. When money containing pure energy is used to fulfil the needs and comforts of your family, the wellbeing of everyone is guaranteed. So if you are employed, strive to do more for your organization than expected. If you run a business, put your customers' gains ahead of yours. Do not give in to any form of unethical means that are passed off as 'normal' by society. Go the extra mile not to get, but to give.

Many of us live by the philosophy of survival of the fittest, which makes life a struggle. Spirituality teaches us that the one who serves is the fittest. It encourages 'Seva Bhav' which means the intention of serving, at every step of life. Our mindset of survival is a barrier to our nature of service. We thought the more we accumulate, the more successful and satisfied we will be. We have accumulated a lot today but feel hollow within because of the void created by going against our nature of serving. Serving does not mean you suppress your aspirations and give all your possessions away. Set goals, earn money, enjoy comforts and achieve everything you can but you can also certainly make it a personal principle to share some of your resources like wealth, knowledge, skills or time. Serve humanity, nature and the world since service is the purpose of life. Shift from an attitude of 'What's in it for me?' to 'What can I do for them?' You can serve with your intentions, thoughts, words, actions, virtues and powers, and these vibrations can influence people. All you need is to be and live your original qualities. If someone is experiencing anger and hatred, your love heals them. If they are in fear or panicking, your peace empowers them. There is no limit to the number of people you can thus heal and empower.

Habit # 6: Change Your Destiny with Every Meal

The pivotal role that food and water play in our lives can never be overstated. But we seem to lack an understanding of certain key aspects of our diet. There are two popular sayings: 'As is the food, so is the mind' and 'You are what you eat'. We know, we understand and we believe in them. But we do not seem to implement this wisdom. A healthy and balanced diet is not only about organic preparation, nutrients and calories. Scientific evidence shows how food alters our emotional health. The food we eat and the water we drink have vibrations, and therefore they affect our emotional state. They directly influence our thoughts, feelings and personality. They are the simplest ways to raise our vibration or lower it.

Let us pay attention to these three aspects during every meal.

1: Switch to a Vegetarian Diet

Along with physical nutrients, we must take care of the vibrations of food. We are aware that animals are kept in a poor condition in slaughterhouses. An animal is also a soul, so it creates emotions like stress, fear, pain, aggression, hatred, helplessness, anxiety, hurt and violence just before death. The emotions of a slaughtered animal affect its body, so along with low emotional energy, even the body of the animal will have low energy. Thus, non-vegetarian food has low vibrational energy and it impacts our mind and body when we consume such food.

After attending a cremation ritual, the first thing we do is take a shower. Why do we do that? To cleanse ourselves of negative vibrations. It is also a custom to not cook food at home as long as a dead body is kept at home, since we do not want food to absorb vibrations of grief and pain. Think about this: We do not cook or eat in a house where the dead body of a dear family member is kept. Then why do we consume the dead body (of an animal or bird) in the name of health? A non-vegetarian diet might have essential proteins and vitamins, but it also has vibrations of aggression, fear, hatred, violence, pain and death. Such food is not right for our emotional health. Moreover, vegetarian alternatives rich in essential proteins and vitamins are available. Today, the medical fraternity across the world is suggesting that a non-vegetarian diet is not the best for our physical health too.

We need a diet that is high in life force, such as a vegetarian diet. This raises a question: do plants not feel pain when we pluck vegetables or fruits for consumption? It helps to understand that there is a huge difference between animal life and plant life. Both undoubtedly have life but their relationship and purpose in life are different. When animals are confronted, they use their mobility or attacking skills to save themselves. That is why they are forcibly captured and held captive in slaughterhouses. The presence of the central nervous system causes them pain when they are harmed. We also understand that once an animal is even partly disabled or if its organ is cut, it cannot regrow that part. The animal is either permanently disabled or may not even survive thereafter.

Plants and trees do not feel pain when they are cut, as they do not have a nervous system. Besides, plants themselves do not have a need for their fruits or vegetables. That is why we see fruits, vegetables and flowers fall to the ground naturally. If the falling would have caused them pain, a plant would not let them drop. Plants also have the ability to regrow any part that is cut. So even if vegetables, flowers, fruits, branches, leaves or seeds are plucked, the plant regrows them and continues to flourish. In some cases, a seed or stem which is dropped on the ground springs into a new plant within a few days. This is how plant life is designed. So, there is no harm caused to them. And there is good reason to consider a plant-based diet as safe, pure and healthy.

2: Commit to Emotional Hygiene

You might have experienced the difference between these three: food bought from outside, food cooked at home and sanctified food (prasad) cooked at places of worship. There is not only a difference in taste but also in their vibrations. The intentions, environment and state of mind of the person cooking, directly influence the food being cooked.

In a restaurant, food is prepared and sold with the intention of maximizing profits. So, a want or a lack of money becomes the predominant energy trapped in the food cooked there. Such food is also likely to have vibrations of stress, fatigue and hurry. Besides, the food absorbs vibrations of all the conversations taking place at the restaurant. It is good to avoid eating in a public place unless there is no other option.

Eat homecooked food and take that food to your workplace as well. Food cooked at home is infused with vibrations of love and nurturing for the family. So never cook unwillingly. Remember that you are not doing an ordinary task. You are nurturing the minds and bodies of your family, influencing their sanskars and their destiny. Even if you are angry or upset, sit in silence for a few minutes, sort out your thoughts and silence your mind before cooking. If you are getting late, choose to cook fewer and simpler dishes but do it with ease, enjoying the experience of nurturing. Always be aware that more than nutrients, it is your vibration that has a stronger impact on the minds of those partaking in the meal. Do not have the TV or radio playing in the background. Abstain from gossip, criticism, judgement or any other form of negativity while cooking.

Convert every meal cooked at home into prasad by cooking in a pure, meditative state. Place a speaker in the kitchen and have spiritual songs or discourses playing throughout the day. With this, not just your mind but everything in the kitchen—pulses, fruits, vegetables, water—get energized with pure vibrations. Many of us cook this way on special occasions. Let us make this our normal way of cooking, so that everyone who eats it will experience calm and healing energy on a daily basis.

3: Eat Mindfully

There is a common complaint that food today is not providing us as much nutrition as it is supposed to. This might not always (or entirely) be true. Often, food has the energy it is meant to give but the state of mind of the person eating becomes questionable. Today, most of us have a hurried breakfast, a working lunch at office and dinner while socializing or watching TV. Food is sacred, so mealtimes should be considered a ritual and not just another activity to tick off the list.

Mindful eating enables us to eat on time, at a set place, making right choices about what to eat and how much to eat. It also lets us eat slowly and attentively enough to enjoy the meal on the plate. Distracted eating happens when our mind is elsewhere as we eat—watching TV, using the phone, reading something, finishing up office work or having wrong conversations. Not paying attention to a meal often leads to overeating. Moreover, food absorbs vibrations, so it will absorb whatever you watch, read, listen or speak while eating. Make it a habit at home to stay away from gadgets while eating. If adults practise it, children will follow. Do not have gadgets on the dining table. When eating at the workplace, ensure that your mind is calm and not working, thinking or talking about work. Have meetings before or after the meal, not while eating because otherwise the mind becomes engaged in other conversations. Remember that it is not only the body which has to eat but the mind needs to be present as well. If you are socializing over dinner, take care that you sit down for those fifteen minutes and have only pure and positive conversations.

The adage, 'A family that eats together stays together' is worth recalling in this context. It means when food has vibrations of love and care, the minds of a family that consumes that food get influenced in the same direction. Their thoughts, words and actions promote harmony. Discuss problems or issues either before or after the meal but never during the meal. Also, do not create thoughts of dislike, displeasure and criticism or comment on someone's health or dietary choices while eating. Food traps these vibrations too. It is beneficial to state the ten affirmations just before you eat. You may say them either as a silent prayer or say them aloud together as a family, so that even children make it a habit. Eat with a silent mind or have happy conversations.

Just for three months, experiment with a plant-based diet, home-cooked food, mindful eating, eating while having only happy conversations and stating affirmations. You will certainly experience a significant shift in the energy of your mind and body.

Habit # 7: Ease into Deep and Restful Sleep

- *I was dozing off but she messaged me at midnight so we chatted till 2 a.m.*
- *All-night parties are so much fun. I never miss them.*
- *I am a night owl. I remain up till late night to study as I cannot wake up before 8 a.m.*
- *I don't have time during the day so I binge-watch shows at night.*
- *I went to bed on time but started browsing social media. Before I realized, it was midnight.*

These are just a few reasons we cite for not sleeping well. Often, not going to bed on time is not circumstantial; it is due to a lack of self-discipline. Nothing can replace a good night's sleep when it comes to healing and rejuvenation. Sleep can be compared to a computer rebooting and refreshing. Usually, sleep is closely associated with physical rest, although it has an equal, if not bigger, impact on our emotional wellbeing. A variety of sleep disorders are prevalent across all age groups. Using medications to induce or aid sleep is commonplace. Persistent lack of sleep and poor quality of sleep have led to sleep deprivation. This has either caused or aggravated a host of unhealthy sanskars we are working to overcome, such as confusion, lack of focus, sluggishness, impatience, irritation and stress. This is a sign that our attitude towards sleep needs to change and change quickly.

Some of us do spend the last five minutes of the day meditating or listening to soft music to fall asleep. But that is not always enough. The mind does not switch off as soon as we switch off lights at bedtime. It is not designed to go from full-fledged activity to slumber in a matter of five minutes. Good sleep hygiene entails a proper mental detox and winding down.

Answer these questions:

- How long does it typically take you to fall asleep?
- Are you often tempted to hit snooze when the alarm goes off and go back to sleep?
- Do you fall asleep during the day, especially when travelling?

If you are driving a car in the fifth gear and need to stop, you do not bring the gear to neutral directly and apply the brake. You shift the gear first, bringing it to the fourth, third, second, first, and then to neutral, before braking. The same holds true for the mind. Having created thousands of thoughts all day long, the mind cannot just fall asleep the moment you lie down. It first needs to be slowed down.

You may follow these guidelines to experience deep sleep.

1. Sleep early to wake up early. Stick to the same sleep schedule even on weekends and holidays. The highest energizing time is said to be from 10 p.m. to 4 a.m. Remaining asleep during this time window enhances immunity, creativity, intuition power, clarity and decision-making. We all know someone who sleeps for ten hours at night but wakes up feeling lethargic. We also know someone who sleeps for just five hours but remains energetic throughout the next day. So, it is not the duration alone but the time when you fall asleep sleep also matters. Rework your routine to get into bed before 10 p.m. Do not let your mind give excuses.

2. Disconnect from work communication at least two hours before bedtime.
   a) Before technology came along in a big way, our mind used to be connected with family after work hours. Today, our mind remains connected to our work, until or even beyond bedtime. Do not engage in emails, calls or messages relating to work after 8 p.m. unless it is urgent.
   b) Reading about work-related issues just before sleep stimulates your mind to keep thinking about it for a long time. An already tired mind feels more fatigued. It implies even when your body is rested at night, the mind remains at work.

c) Do not just stay logged in to work just because your colleagues do so. Trust yourself and do not copy others. Instead of working late, wake up early and work at the time of highest intuition and efficiency. With less time and effort, you will get more results. Be the one creating the change. Soon your co-workers will also implement these practices. If you head a team or organization, insist or make it a rule that all forms of work communication stop by 8 p.m.

d) Delineating work hours from personal time allows your mind to withdraw from a fully engaged state and naturally slow down as you go to bed.

3. Detox from gadgets at least an hour before bedtime to slow down your mind.

a) Abstain from emotionally stimulating content like news, movies, serials, crime shows or loud music.

b) Turn off notifications or set your smartphone on silent. Keep it away from your bed and do not use it until morning, no matter what. Otherwise, even if you take a peek, you might be tempted to respond to notifications. One message leads to another, one click leads to another, one app leads to another ... and an entire hour might pass before you know it.

c) Unplugging from screens not only makes room for inner silence but also limits eye strain.

4. Spend five minutes to resolve any issue on your mind to slow it down before bedtime.

a) The mind is like a curious little child who keeps asking questions and often projects unnecessary information. Check if your mind is mulling over any question or issue. Handle it patiently and give answers to silence it.

b) Even if you do not have a solution, say to your mind, 'Let us think about this tomorrow. Everything is perfect and will always be. Time to sleep now.' Besides, when you wake up fresh and think with an energized mind, you are more likely to find the optimal solution.

c) The subconscious mind keeps working even when you are asleep. What it works on depends on your thoughts just before you drift into sleep. If problems are your last thoughts, your mind cannot rest or recharge through the night.

5. Write in a journal for five minutes to dump your thoughts and clear your mind. Journalling also enables reflection, learning and improvement. Rewind the day and look at the experiences that you feel were significant:

a) If you had a negative experience, jot it down briefly to clear the load of negativity. Do not focus on the situation or people involved. Ask yourself, 'Could I have responded differently?' Write down what the right response would have been. Visualize yourself responding that way so it gets recorded in the subconscious mind. This prepares your mind for the future.

b) Forgive people who were not right to you, regardless of their role, position or mistake. Release negative impressions you created about them, understanding that they had a different perspective, they were disturbed or it was a return of a past karmic account.

c) Intentionally or unintentionally, you might have made mistakes. If you did not get a chance to apologize, you can now seek forgiveness mentally. Do not create guilt or shame. Love and forgive yourself to get the strength to move on. Your vibrations reach the other person and the relationship starts healing.

d) Celebrate your small and big wins by writing about the situations where you used compassion, kindness or forgiveness or engaged in good acts. Appreciate yourself to feel inspired to repeat them more often.

e) You may also write a few words of gratitude for everything that went well that day and to be thankful for the people, objects, places or tasks that were a part of it.

6. Consume spiritual or self-transformational content for ten to fifteen minutes, similar to the morning routine. Its vibrations of purity, compassion, faith and acceptance will get processed while you are asleep. For the next five minutes, repeat the ten affirmations or write them in your diary before you sleep. The content you create or consume during these fifteen minutes get embedded in your subconscious mind and radiate to your body for the next six hours. Remember that recordings on the subconscious mind are what eventually become your sanskars. Besides, the pure vibrations radiating to every cell of your body manifests health.

This simple nightly routine promotes deeper sleep and you will eventually require less sleep. So you will effectively save nearly two hours on a daily basis.

Let the Action Begin ...

With approximately sixty to seventy-five minutes a day, you can re-energize yourself, seize the day and overcome any adversity with peace and stability. These seven practices make all the difference between operating at your peak potential and wrestling with a disturbed mind to complete your tasks. Experiment with them and see how they elevate your state of being. Begin with one week and you will gain the motivation to continue for another week, then the next week and the next ... it will soon become a normal part of life. As you start giving a meaningful structure to your days and start making time for healthy activities, your mind and body will thank you.

Do not put this off for a weekend, your birthday or the New Year. Begin today and be consistent. Let there be no excuses, no fears and no delays. There could be (read: will be) days when you slip up—perhaps you wake up at 7 a.m. or miss the traffic control of thoughts or sleep late. Never mind. It is important that you do not give up. Persist with discipline to evolve into a happier and healthier self. Follow the routines consistently to a point where it becomes impossible to *not* follow them.

12

Destiny: A Matter of Choice or Chance?

A FUNDRAISER WAS ORGANIZED AT AN OFFICE TO RAISE money for an orphanage, so a donation box was circulated among the staff gathered in the auditorium. One of the employees took out an old, soiled and taped 100-rupee note from his pocket, folded it quickly and slipped into the donation box. Grinning wryly, he thought, 'I got rid of that mutilated note. No one would have accepted it anyway. Besides, I appeared charitable in front of everyone'. Just then, his friend tapped on his shoulder and handed him 2,000 rupees. The employee took it and dropped it into the donation box on behalf of his friend.

Later that day the employee said to his friend, 'That was generous of you to donate 2,000 rupees.' His friend smiled, 'Come on! That was your money, not mine. I saw it falling from your pocket so I just picked and gave it to you.'

The employee felt terrible. He simply stood staring at his friend in disbelief. It took him a few moments to realize and say, 'That was my karma hitting back.'

All of us make plans about how we want our life and the lives of our family and friends to be. We also write a script in our minds of what we want to do and how to go about it. Most events go according to our mental script and at times, they turn out even better. However, there are moments when one unexpected event stands before us, changing everything for the worse. In those moments, the first thought our mind asks is, 'Why did this happen to me? What wrong have I done to deserve this?'

We come across several incidents that seem hard to reconcile with:

- An excellent driver succumbs to a road accident, while the reckless driver who caused it escapes unhurt.
- A sincere employee does not get the recognition he deserves. His colleague who often shies away from duties gets rewarded.
- An investor loses millions in the stock market in a matter of hours. The same day, a daily-wage worker wins the one crore jackpot prize on a lottery ticket.

Who is deciding the course of events in our life, day after day after day?

Is Your Destiny in God's Hands?

'Where was God when this was happening?' is a common phrase we hear or say in times of adversity. This is because of the belief that God or the Creator is deciding all our life experiences.

Recall how many times you hear or even yourself say, 'This was God's will, so we need to accept it.'

Even as children we were taught that God is watching us constantly. And that He will either reward us or punish us, based on our deeds. We believed it is God who can rectify the situation when something is not going right in our life. This is why we had been asking God for this and that and the other: 'Please change my life … Please give me some peace … Please make me rich … Please cure my illness … Please get me this job …' We kept lining up requests one after the other. Sometimes our prayers were answered and sometimes not. Surprisingly, we never paused to validate if it is God who decides our destiny. Now will be a good time to examine.

Firstly, if God was writing our destiny as He willed, how would our life be? Perfect. Just as you would write nothing short of perfect for your children, God also cannot let His children go through the slightest discomfort. After all, He is our Supreme Parent.

Secondly, if God was writing our destiny, how would each of our destinies be?

- Will every individual experience the same extent of peace, love and happiness? Yes.
- Will every individual be equally healthy and live a long life? Yes.
- Will every individual have the same amount of wealth and material comfort? Yes.

God as a parent cannot write unequal destinies for His children. He cannot be prejudiced towards anyone, just as you would not favour one of your children over the other.

Now, look at your life. Have you ever felt sad or hurt? Did you have an issue with your health? Have you had conflicts in your relationships? Have you faced challenges in your career? Most likely, our answer is a 'yes' for at least one of these. This means our destiny has not been perfect. Next, look at the world around you. One infant is born perfectly healthy and another is born with an illness. One person lives in a mansion while another lives on the street. Someone is pampered by the entire family while another is orphaned. This means our destinies are not equal. Since our destiny is neither perfect nor equal, it is logical to conclude that God does not decide our destiny.

Can You Decide Your Destiny?

There is another popular belief we grew up with: everything that happens to me is a consequence of my karma. Let us evaluate it. We all create beautiful karmas but at times we do make mistakes. Since our karmas are not perfect, our destiny is also not perfect. Besides, our karmas are not identical and hence our destinies are not equal. So it is logical to conclude that our karmas decide our destiny.

You may recall the flow:

Thoughts – Feelings – Attitude – Action – Habit/Sanskar – Personality – Destiny

So, destiny is whatever we choose to create. One thought can change our destiny by taking us in the right direction or a wrong one.

This raises a question about God's role in our life. God is just like a parent. Parents are constantly present to support us. They advise, guide, love and empower us ... but they cannot control our karma. Children are creators of their own karma and they receive consequences accordingly. Similarly, God who is our Supreme Parent, gives us knowledge, love and power to do what is right. It is up to us to take them, empower ourselves and engage in right karmas.

Suppose a person does not take care of his body for ten years. He does not exercise, does not control his diet, eats junk food regularly, sleeps after midnight and wakes up late. Because of this negligence, his body falls ill. If he were to ask, 'Why did I fall ill?', where should he point the finger of blame? At himself. And if he were to ask, 'Who can heal me now?', where should he point his finger? At himself. Through his wrong actions, he wrote a destiny of illness. Now with his right actions of caring for his body, he can create health. So his destiny is his choice and his creation.

The equation is the same for all of us. Everything good that is happening in our life and everything that is not so good, come about only because of the karmas we have carried out. Nothing is excluded. The consequences of our good karmas come as pleasant experiences. The consequences of our wrong karmas come as challenging experiences. **At every step of life, our karma writes our destiny.** We have the freedom to make our own choices about the karma that we will engage in. This is called free will. It is like holding a pen and writing our own destiny. In simple terms, if life is a game, the Law of Karma lays down the rules to play it. If we use our free will to play by the rules, we will emerge as winners in every scene of life.

The Karmic Interplay

The Law of Karma is not new to most of us. Originating from Sanskrit, the word 'karma' means action. The Law of Karma states that our every action is a karma which has an equal consequence, manifesting as our destiny. The law is also known by other names like the Law of Cause and Effect or the Law of Action and Reaction. The concepts of this law are also conveyed proverbially as 'As you sow, so shall you reap' and 'What goes around comes around'. For several centuries, every religion across the world has prescribed concepts, doctrines or guidelines aligning with the Law of Karma. Yet, it often seems like we disregard its workings and go about our lives, doing what we want to. Ignorance of the law does not exempt us from facing karmic consequences.

Suppose your behaviour with someone is courteous and your words are polite. You might see that as perfect karma. But what you fail to see is that your thoughts about that person are critical and judgemental. If you are irritated, hurt or unhappy about that person, what energy do you create? Your negative thoughts easily exceed and overpower your right words and behaviours. That relationship will remain fragile until you start thinking right too. You made efforts only on the visible karma but the invisible powerful karma of intentions and thoughts will bring back unpleasant consequences in the form of that person's behaviour or reactions. You might not understand why, despite your right behaviour, things are not smooth. The truth is that karma begins with thoughts.

Our mind is not only where our karma is 'first' created but is also where 'maximum' karma is created, as our thoughts outnumber our words and actions. Each time you create a karma, it brings back not one but four consequences.

- Firstly, your karma influences your state of mind. If you create a thought of love, it is your karma and you feel nice as the consequence of that karma. If you create a thought of anger, you will feel its consequence as a disturbance in your state of mind.
- Secondly, your karma influences your body. If you hold on to hurt or resentment for, say ten years, that energy keeps radiating to your body. The body will obviously show consequences.
- Thirdly, your karma influences your relationships. If you create a respectful thought for someone, it immediately reaches the other person as a vibration. As a consequence, that person creates a similar quality of energy which travels back to you.
- Fourthly, your karma influences the environment. If you create a thought of kindness, it radiates and raises the collective vibration of the world.

Energy that we create as invisible intentions, thoughts and feelings, as well as our visible behaviours, are all vibrations that we create and radiate. This is our karma. Situations that unfold in our life as our health, finances, career, relationships, people's behaviours—basically anything coming to us from outside—is the energy we receive. This is our destiny. In a nutshell:

- Energy we create = Karma
- Energy we receive = Destiny

The Law of Karma explains how karma and destiny are interconnected. The energy that we send out will be the quality of the energy that will return to us. Let us consider energy to be a ball.

- Karma would be the ball we throw out. The direction, speed and angle of the throw is completely our choice.
- Destiny is like a boomerang, where the ball returns to us. The return journey of the ball is not at all in our control. It comes back exactly based on how we had thrown it. So now we cannot escape or avoid the ball on its return journey.

Do We Have Free Will or Is It All Predestined?

Karma is as fascinating as it is intriguing. And it creates a lot of curious questions in our minds. We have heard these two diametrically opposite beliefs often:

- *Everything is predestined.*
- *I have the free will to create my destiny.*

These two lines confuse us. They bring up a pertinent question: if we are the creators of our destiny, it means we are writing our future on a blank page—new and fresh. But if everything is predestined, then what are we writing?

Interestingly, both the lines are true. When a child is born, it is customary in many families to get an astrological chart made. The chart predicts significant happenings in regard to health, career, marriage, success, lifespan and so on. The child is just born, so it seems logical that he is yet to create karmas or write his destiny. How can someone already predict his future? This is because a significant part of our destiny is predestined. But by whom? Destiny is predestined by the creator of the karmas.

When we create intentions and thoughts, when we speak and behave, it appears as if it is this body which is doing it all. But now we know that our body is only an instrument through which the soul comes into action. So our every karma is created by the soul, not by the body. We have already internalized that sanskars are recorded on the soul. Every soul carries five types of sanskars, one of them being the sanskars of the past births. These sanskars have a significant bearing on our present life. When the body is no longer able to function, the soul, which is eternal, moves forward on its journey. It leaves behind everything it has acquired and carries forward everything it has created. The soul moves forward on the journey with its sanskars and karmas and enters the womb of the mother. After a few months, the baby is born with the sanskars and karmas it has carried. This is why destiny is 'pre-written'.

Let us go back to the analogy of considering energy to be a ball. When a person throws the karma ball, the consequence or destiny ball can return to him within a few seconds, a few minutes, few months or after several years. In the meantime, suppose the soul changes its bodily costume. Since the person has already thrown the karmic ball, it is bound to return as destiny. When we create the karma, we write our destiny at the same moment. For us, it seems like a matter of life, death and new birth. But for the soul it is simply a change of costume.

Suppose a person borrows 5,000 rupees from his friend. He is wearing a blue dress today. Tomorrow when he changes into a brown dress, does he need to return the amount?

Answer: obviously, yes.

He cannot escape saying that his dress has changed. For, the dress did not borrow money. The person borrowed the money.

What if three years later, he leaves the body, which means he changes his physical costume? Will he still need to return the money?

Answer: obviously, yes.

He cannot avoid it saying the transaction had happened in the previous birth and has nothing to do with the present. The body had not borrowed money. The person had borrowed it. So the soul owes it back.

The only issue is that after changing the bodily costume, he will not remember the past birth, let alone the fact that he owes 5,000 rupees to his friend. But destiny will bring them in a situation where the money will have to be returned, even if his friend has also changed his body. Although it sounds complicated, it is quite simple. Take a minute to think about it. Perhaps a lot of questions of life will get answered. While one cannot pinpoint the exact scenario, here is a sample incident to get an understanding of how the Law of Karma works. Early one morning, that person who had borrowed 5,000 rupees in his previous lifetime, sets out for work. He takes his car out and just as he makes a turn, his car bumps into a bike parked by the side, causing a dent. The owner of the bike not only abuses him but also demands a compensation of 5,000 rupees. The former reluctantly hands over the money and the whole day, keeps pondering why it happened when he was so good at driving and had driven around that same spot thousands of times. He creates a series of thoughts: 'Maybe if I had left the house two minutes later, I would have avoided it … What if I had taken the other road … What if I had worked from home today … What if …'

But it had to happen exactly that way. The karmic ball had to return. He had to return the money—exactly 5,000 rupees—to his erstwhile friend, although he does not remember borrowing it. Memories get erased when the soul leaves the bodily costume but karmas are recorded and will need to be settled. So, returning the money was predestined—by the person himself, on the day he borrowed the money. Now, whether he pays the money with ease or feels angry, stressed, hurt or pays out of fear—that is the new karma he will create.

Circling back to the example of the newborn, let us understand that based on the past karmas, situations will progressively arise in the life of the baby. These situations are predestined. In each situation, that baby will choose how to respond to what is happening. This means, what is coming to him is predestined but how he will face them is not. That is his present choice, his present karma.

At the end of every financial year, businesses generate a closing balance sheet. On the very next day, that same balance sheet is treated as the opening balance sheet for the new financial year. Our karmic balance sheet works similarly. Our last moment in the present body determines the closing karmic balance sheet for the present lifetime. When the baby is born, the same balance sheet becomes the opening karmic balance sheet. However, it is extremely important to note that it is only an 'opening balance sheet'. The future course of life depends on the quality of karmas created by that soul in the present life. Even if the opening balance sheet shows a loss of 10 lakh, a smart businessman can run his business so well that he will not only break even but also make a profit of 20 lakh in the current financial year.

Predestined just means a previously written destiny, written by us based on the karma we chose that day. How we respond to that destiny in the present is our free will, our present karma. Our present karma will have a future consequence.

At every moment of our life, three aspects of time are at play:

- The consequence of the **past** karma is coming to us.
- How we respond to it is our **present** karma.
- Our present karma decides our **future** destiny.

The past is the ball returning to us, which is not in our control. How we respond to the situation is our present karma, the new ball that we are throwing out, which is completely in our control. And this new ball will also return, so we are writing our future. Past karmas can be powerful but how we face them now is important. So greater power lies in our present karma.

Predictions: Probability or Reality?

- *I will have a successful career. My horoscope says so.*
- *The next two years are going to be tough as per my horoscope. I am so scared.*
- *I gave up driving because he predicted that I would get involved in an accident.*
- *I will not begin this task today. My horoscope says Wednesday is unlucky for me.*

These are examples of statements people make based on predictions.

Suppose a doctor warns a patient based on genetic factors and present test reports that she might become diabetic in about six months. This is a scientific prediction. Now if she gets worried and starts believing that she will indeed become diabetic and does not do anything significant to change her lifestyle, she might develop diabetes even before six months. But if she takes the warning as a wake-up call, changes her lifestyle, diet and thought patterns, then she might never contract diabetes. The prediction was accurate based on her current lifestyle. But a prediction is only a probability. What she does with that probability creates her reality.

Astrology is a science which predicts certain situations that will unfold in our life. These situations are called our destiny, which got decided (predestined) based on our past karmas. Astrology can predict our destiny because we have already created it, so it is a science of the consequences of our past karmas.

Gently visualize yourself throwing a karmic ball towards a wall in front of you. The ball will hit the wall and return. Throwing the ball was your past karma. The ball returning to you is your present destiny. That returning ball is comparable to a situation in your life. How you choose to respond to the situation—the new ball which you throw now, which is completely in your control—is your present karma. Science can predict your destiny, that is, how the ball will return can be calculated based on how you had thrown it earlier. But science cannot predict how you will throw the new ball.

A situation could be a crisis but in our present karma, if we remain calm and stable, then we cross it with ease. The crisis could be predicted but how we respond will depend on our present sanskars. The crisis has come because of a past wrong karma, which was created because of a negative sanskar at that time. If we have not changed that sanskar, then in the present we will again create a negative response and therefore create suffering. If we have changed the sanskar, we will respond with positivity and cross it with ease.

We have seen how someone panics if they lose 1,000 rupees while another who loses crores in a business remains stable, more determined to start again. It is all about how we react to the situation: while someone complains about a headache, another person might be full of gratitude for each new day in the face of a terminal illness; someone gets upset about getting fewer likes on their social media post, while another forgives even the person who betrayed them; someone might feel sad about their phone screen developing scratches while another remains stable even upon losing a family member. This goes to show that our quality of life does not depend on the magnitude of the problem, but solely on how much suffering we choose to create. Life is not about what happens to us, it is about how we perceive, think, feel and respond to whatever happens to us.

It is not important to know what is going to happen in future. But what is important is to strengthen the self daily to face anything that happens with dignity and stability. We just need to focus on changing any uncomfortable sanskars so we can create the right karma in every scene.

Karma: Keeping It Right All the Time

Suppose two families set out for a picnic. Everyone is having fun—chatting, listening to music, enjoying the view and eating. Their cars cross each other at some point and the drivers create a thought, 'Let us race'. The two cars are inherently different, so it might actually be impossible for one to get ahead of the other. Yet, they decide to race. Once they create this thought, how will the rest of their drive be? It shifts from being fun and enjoyable to one that is stressful and aggressive. The focus shifts from the family to the speed of the other car. The purpose shifts from being a pleasant drive to overtaking the other car. They both run into a traffic signal. And the driver of the car lagging, feels that jumping the traffic signal is an easy way to get ahead. He drives straight through a red light, thereby compromising on rules and risking safety.

Like on the road, even in life, often we just create this thought, 'Life is a competition'. Thereafter starts our stressful journey of wanting to outdo other people. By believing we are the role we perform, we also believe that being ahead in the competition makes us better than other people. The urge to get ahead of others to achieve success at times prompts us to compromise on our values, ethics and principles.

Let us assume you are the driver of the car that is slightly behind in the race. If the car ahead of you breaks down during the so-called race that you have started, will you stop to help? Or since you are in a race, will you look at it as an opportunity to speed past that car and get as far ahead as possible? Do introspect on this scenario. Sometimes, without awareness, we feel glad that the other person is stuck, whether on a road or in life.

Our consciousness creates our belief systems, which in turn create our thoughts and behaviours. These thoughts, words and behaviours are our karmas which create our destiny. Believing ourselves to be a role, position or status creates ego consciousness, which creates a belief system that life is a competition. This false belief thus leads to a chain of wrong karmas that create stress, anxiety, disharmony and disappointment, or lead to a compromise of values and even prioritizing achievements over the self and family. When we choose cooperation over competition, self-esteem over comparison, inspiration over jealousy, patience over irritation, forgiveness over holding on, acceptance over expectations, empathy over aggression, motivation over control, we gradually shift from body-conscious karmas to soul-conscious karmas. Every right karma is soul-strengthening, no matter how insignificant it may seem.

Why Good People Suffer

Everyone engages in an enormous amount of right karma, but at times we create wrong karmas. And when something does not go our way, we cannot map this destiny to its cause. Maybe it is a consequence of a wrong karma we had created in a previous lifetime but the time for its settlement has come now. There is often a time delay between creating our karma and facing its consequence. We fail to make the connection.

Sometimes, we see a person working hard but not getting expected results. But for someone else, success comes effortlessly. We feel it is unfair. But the Law of Karma is always accurate. For instance, consider two equally bright students preparing for an exam to be held in a month's time. One of them studies twelve hours a day while the other studies for five hours daily, plays with friends, spends time with family and generally seems relaxed. People around them expect that the former will perform better. But the opposite happens and the latter scores higher. So everyone raises questions and labels the result as unfair. But a few days later, someone informs them that the student who studied twelve hours a day during the last one month had not studied much previously. But the student who studied only five hours during the last one month had studied systematically throughout the year. Hence, eventually, he was much better prepared. This information clarifies that the result was fair.

Much like this example, we tend to question each other's destiny at times, only because we do not know the other person's previous lifetimes or the whole picture. If there was a way to see our past and everyone else's, it would be straightforward to agree that the Law of Karma delivers impartially to everyone, all the time. It is always fair and accurate.

That leads us towards yet another reason to realize that life is *not* a competition, unlike popular belief. When we compare and compete with someone else, we only see our present parameters. But no two souls have the same past. Even for two souls born as twins, everything in the present could be identical: parents, upbringing, environment, education, resources and so on. Perhaps both are equally intelligent, hardworking and sincere too. This means all their present parameters are the same. So we assume or expect their destiny also to be the same. Now if both of them start businesses within the same locality and sell the same product, they may not necessarily be equally successful. One will be more successful than the other. This is because of one factor which is different: their past karma. **Even if all parameters are identical in the present, there cannot be competition because of different past karmic accounts**. A race is fair only if it has identical parameters. Life is not a competition; we are not in a race. Life is a journey not only of one but many lifetimes. Let us make it a beautiful experience.

By comparing, competing and creating stress, fear, jealousy and dissatisfaction, we create several negative karmas in the present. After all this, even if we manage to somehow get ahead of others, our destiny will still not have happiness and health in store for us because of the depleting emotions we created along the way.

Being Right When You Are Wronged

Is it possible to be nice to someone who is not nice to you? Is it possible to bless someone who has wronged you? Is it possible to trust someone who has betrayed you? Most of us would say no.

Suppose your friend incurs a huge loss with his business venture. Seeing you rise to the top of your career and receiving appreciation, he feels jealous of you. He not only cuts off communication with you but also spreads rumours to taint your image. You feel hurt and angry. What will your thoughts be? Let us do a small exercise:

- Repeat these lines twice: 'Being a friend, how could you speak ill about me? You will face consequences and repent for the pain you have caused me.'
- Now repeat this twice: 'I understand you are in deep pain. You had a reason for what you did. I forgive you. I let go of what happened. I will always be there for you. You are a powerful soul and God's blessings are always with you to bounce back in your business.'

They are two different ways of thinking: the first set is of low-vibration thoughts and the second, high-vibration thoughts. Which set of thoughts are easy? More importantly, which set is the right karma?

When someone is wrong to us, we can choose to remain bitter about that person for a few minutes, days, years or a lifetime. Believing we can never forgive, we live in pain for too long. Some of us even make strong statements like, 'I will not forgive them till I die.' But we now understand that hurt is an emotion created by the soul, not by the body. So if our pain is not released and healed, the soul will carry it into the next lifetime.

Think about this: when we leave the body, all these are left behind—people who wronged us, their mistakes, everyone involved in the situation and their reactions. The only entity that gets carried forward with us are the emotions we created in response to their mistakes. It is the soul with an unhealed wound which will take a new bodily costume in a few months. This means in the next lifetime, your family could be very caring and external situations could be perfect, but you the soul are carrying a past wound of hurt. Hence, the slightest unpleasantness can trigger pain. If you know people who get hurt easily, it could be because they have carried the pain from a previous life along with other sanskars and karmas.

Let us internalize the energy equations. People who misbehave or are wrong to us are not in their best emotional health in those moments. They are at a lower vibrational energy, which has led them to behave that way. Let us call it an emotional disease. If we feel upset or hurt, it means we are lowering our emotional immunity and catching their infection. Our emotional disturbance lowers our vibrations and we get influenced by their energies. This means they created a wrong karma by harming us and then we created a wrong karma by creating hurt. We normally believe that only that person—and not us—has created wrong karma. That is false because wrong karma means any thought, word or behaviour which lowers our vibrations. Wrong karma also means any emotion which depletes soul power. By creating hurt in response to their behaviour, we have also created wrong karma. Cheating, betraying, abusing, lying, dominating, controlling and criticizing are, no doubt, wrong karmas. But creating hurt, rejection, insecurity, guilt and self-criticism or feeling unwanted in response to what happens to us also amounts to wrong karma by us.

When someone wrongs us, our first step should be to protect ourselves emotionally. This comes with the understanding that their karmas reflect their sanskar and their present state of mind. They are emotionally unwell. And their behaviour is not about us but about who they are in the present moment. So, let us never say, 'She did this TO ME.' The 'to me' part can leave us unnecessarily vulnerable. Instead, let us pause and counsel our mind to think right: 'She did this because of her sanskar. What she did is her karma, how I respond is my karma. My karma does not depend on what someone else did, it depends on who I am, what sanskars I carry. Their karma creates their destiny, my karma creates mine. I choose the right karma irrespective of who they are and what they did.'

'Why Did that Happen to Me?'

Has it happened to you that even when you did something with a pure intention for someone, it backfired? Your efforts went unnoticed or they expected way more than what you did, or worse, they were upset about what you did. This can happen with people in our closest circle and in friendships, and we feel disappointed. So we question our fate as we cannot figure out what we did to deserve it.

Suppose your best friend starts avoiding you, hardly talks to you and makes new friends. But when you ask her why, she claims that all is well. How will you react? Perhaps you go through a spectrum of negative emotions, from irritation, anger, anxiety, insecurity, worry about losing her, and pain. Finally, a day comes when she breaks up with you, ending years of friendship. You might feel so terrible that you burst into tears, shout at her, resolve to not see her again, cannot forgive her and you even lose faith in friendships. You believe these reactions to be normal. But those are the moments when you need to hold the Law of Karma like a guiding compass, to understand why she behaved that way and how you need to respond.

Remember that people's behaviour towards you, whether they are being kind, honest, lying, betraying, helping or harming—whatever they do—is nothing but energy targeted at you. Let us go back to the energy ball analogy to analyse the karmic dynamics.

- Your friend lied and betrayed you. Let us call that energy a dark-coloured ball that she has sent you. The first thought your mind creates would be, 'Why did she do this to me?'
- Remember that the dark-coloured ball could not have come unless you had sent it out sometime in the past, either in this or a previous lifetime. Knowingly or out of ignorance, a wrong karma was committed in the past.

- You might not be able stop an array of thoughts such as, 'Let alone doing wrong to her, I have never created a single wrong thought about her. I trusted her more than I trusted myself. I always cared for her.' Remember that your karmas were not created by your body, they were created by you, the soul. You do not remember when that happens. Her lies and betrayal are consequences of that past karma, perhaps from an earlier lifetime.

- When we send a dark-coloured ball to someone, it may come back to us in one hour, after ten years or after hundred years. If it comes back after an hour or even after ten years, we are likely to remember that we had thrown it sometime. But if it comes back after hundred years, we, as souls, would have changed our bodily costume. We will therefore neither remember the person nor the reason for their unpleasant behaviour. So we wonder, 'Why did this happen to me?'

- Notice that our mind seldom questions pleasant events in life. It usually takes them for granted. But in the face of challenges like health issues, relationship conflicts, problems at workplace or any other crisis, the mind questions, 'Why is this happening?' There is just one answer: our past karma.

- Just as the Law of Gravity works all the time, the Law of Karma is accurate and persistent. It is a self-sustaining mechanism that needs no monitoring. So, we cannot create questions on anything happening in life. Every incident is accurate, exactly how it is meant to be. This understanding ends the blame game. Once we stop blaming other people or situations, we save a lot of our energy. We shift from being a victim to becoming a master of the situation.

- Visualize the dark balls coming from your friend and see them as balls on a return journey. Those dark balls are not in your control. You want her to realize her mistakes, apologize and change. But her behaviour is not in your control. However, the way you think, speak and behave in response is completely your choice. Your response is your present karma.

- Observe the energy flow: her behaviour is a return of your past karma. Your response is your present karma, which will decide your future or destiny. If you focus on her mistakes, you will only create thoughts of pain and anger. These thoughts will be your new karmic dark balls that you throw at her. You had thrown dark balls earlier, so she is returning them to you. If you continue to throw the same quality of energy (dark balls) towards her even now, you are bound to receive it back once again. This is how we could go on getting entangled in negative karmic accounts with other souls, not just in one lifetime but across several lifetimes.

Let us get a bigger picture of karmic consequences. Suppose you meet someone this evening and your conversation unexpectedly turns into an argument and ends on a bitter note. Next week, you bump into the same person again. That second meeting will begin on a bitter note, with the same negative vibration at which the first meeting ended. You will be cold to each other and create negative thoughts. A month later, you meet for the third time at a public function. That meeting could be much worse. You might get into an ugly spat, talk ill about each other or create a scene in front of other people. Note how every subsequent meeting is going to get more complex and more negative until one of you decides to change the quality of your interaction. It takes one person to brush ego aside, delete the past, forgive the other person and make a new beginning. When one of the two does this, the vibration of the interaction changes. The energy that was spiralling downwards, now starts rising up.

Extrapolate this analogy across multiple lifetimes and you will clearly see that the relationship will only become more and more toxic in every meeting in every lifetime. All it takes is for one of you to change the energy of the ball that you will throw—and YOU can be the one to do this. Think about it like this, you had thrown a dark-coloured ball, which that person is returning. But now you have the choice and chance to throw white (positive) energy balls—in other words, you have the choice of changing the energy of the karmic account you have with that person.

Clearly, being good to people who wrong us, being respectful to people who are rude or being kind to those who are putting obstacles in our path, does not mean we are doing them a favour. Not at all. We are not doing anything for others, we are doing everything only for our own karmic benefit. We are doing it to create a beautiful karma in the present by throwing the white ball, so that a white ball returns to us in the future. Knowing who or what is the cause of our troubles (our own past wrong karmas), makes it easier to be kind, compassionate, stop blaming, radiate blessings and good wishes and thereby settle karmic accounts.

Another important aspect is that when you are nice to people, do not expect a white ball to return from them immediately, just because you have thrown a white one to them. We have no idea how many dark balls we had thrown at someone in the past: it could be just one or it could be a thousand of them. All of them should return, by law. But the greater the number of white balls you throw, the lesser will be the impact of the past dark balls on your mind and your life. While throwing the white balls, you will experience calm and peace, your body feels healthy, your aura vibrates at a divine energy, your life feels perfect even though situations in your life are tough.

Settle Your Karmic Debts

Often we have dark-coloured balls coming from people who are close to us. Children being disobedient, frequent conflicts between a couple, siblings fighting over property, children not taking care of elderly parents … a lot can happen at home. That is when the mind raises questions.

We expect our family to always love and respect us. But let us look at them beyond the labels of relationships. They are souls on a journey just as we are. Today, if we have a negative energy exchange, it must have started in a past lifetime. So, it is not right to question, 'How can my child do this?' or 'How could my husband say that?' They are souls with whom we have interacted in a previous life. Today, they have come into this role with us only because of a strong karmic account we had created at that time. **Let us bear in mind that both positive and negative karmic accounts will accrue in close relationships.** Shifting from role or relationship consciousness to soul consciousness helps us to see this clearly, and thereafter it becomes easy to choose the right karmas.

Regardless of how the other person is, how their words or behaviours are, or what the situation is, we will need to send only white balls, which means the highest vibrations. While sending vibrations of blessings, forgiving, letting go or being nice to someone who has wronged us, it is very important to remember why we are doing so. We are sending a white ball for our own benefit. We are not forgiving them; we are forgiving ourselves. We are being merciful and kind to ourselves, understanding that it was a consequence of our past karmic account. This time, we need to change that karmic account and make a new beginning, write a new destiny based on our karma.

Suppose you draw a dark circle on a paper. If you want to delete that dark circle, how many white circles should you draw over the dark one to make the dark one invisible? Not one or two … perhaps at least eight to ten white circles will remove the trace of a single dark circle. The dark circle corresponds to the unpleasant past memories we have held on to. The white circle corresponds to pure thoughts of blessings and good wishes that we create now for the other person. For every wrong they do, we need to send several blessings, so that their dark energy will not reach us. Besides, the white energy we create at present will start healing our emotional wounds of dark circles we had created in the past. Blessings are healing energy. Instead of consuming their pain, we can heal them with pure vibrations. Meditation and sending focused blessings can finish our past karmic accounts.

Let us say a person feels rejected by her family. She often thinks, 'Everyone rejects me. I was rejected by so-and-so, then by so-and-so ... I have always been rejected.' This rejection is her emotional wound. And by creating such negative thoughts, she will not only deepen the wound but also create more wrong karma with her family. To erase this dark circle of rejection, what will be the white circle? She can say to herself: 'I am a pure soul. I am a loveful soul. I love myself and accept myself unconditionally. I love people and accept them unconditionally. People love me and accept me unconditionally. God loves and accepts me unconditionally.'

These thoughts, when repeated for a few days, will wipe away the feeling of being rejected. This means by changing our karma, we changed our destiny. We also changed our karmic account with people whom we believe had rejected us. When we hold onto any pain, we are connected to people with an energy of pain. If one of us releases the pain and sends blessings, the karmic account changes. Let us be that one person.

People get past life regression therapy done, especially when they go through repetitive negative emotional patterns for a long time. Knowing what transpired in the past brings acceptance of the present in most cases. However, we do not need to know what had happened because even if we get to know everything, the acceptance and healing needs to be done now, in the present. Simply having the awareness that we had an unpleasant past and today we can change the present is sufficient for us to begin healing. Suppose while reading this book, you notice a stain on your dress. You do not know how it got stained but you do not waste time looking for someone to blame for it. You immediately wash it and remove the stain. It is the same with our emotional wounds and the wounds we have inflicted on others; we just need to heal them.

If you are experiencing pain because someone was wrong to you, it is time to change that karmic account by healing yourself and that person. Understanding past karmas makes us realize that their mistake was only because we had wronged them in the past. Neither of us might remember the past but the fact remains that today's situation is a consequence of the past. We are the cause and therefore we must apologize first. It might sound a little uncomfortable at first, but it is only logical. We need to apologize to those who are wrong to us. We do not have to do it in words, we only need to send blessings for healing to begin at that moment.

Blessings means sending healing energy. So there are five steps to heal ourselves and them:

Step 1: Apologize for the pain we have caused them in the past, though we do not remember details.
Step 2: Forgive them for their present behaviour.
Step 3: Release the past.
Step 4: Close the present karmic account energy.
Step 5: Start a beautiful new karmic account.

You can create the healing thoughts and radiate this energy at least twice a day—morning and night—or each time you feel hurt or upset. To begin, every night before going to bed, you could write a message such as this in your personal diary:

I am a powerful soul. I am a pure soul. I apologize for the pain I have caused you in the past. I am sorry. I forgive you for your present behaviour. I understand why you are being this way. I release the past … I forgive … I forget … I let go. The past has passed … it is over … full stop. The past karmic account is over. I now create only love and blessings for you. I accept you. I respect you. You accept me. You respect me. Our new karmic account of trust and respect has begun. God's powers and blessings are a circle of protection around us.

After a few days, you will feel better emotionally, because white circles would have faded or erased the dark circles drawn in the past. This is coding of the mind with right thinking and changing your present karma to white energy balls. You can then skip the thoughts of apology and forgiveness, and continue with the thoughts of releasing the past and creating a beautiful present. You might wonder how just a small set of thoughts repeated for a few days can resolve issues and settle past karmic accounts. The answer is simple: it is only our wrong thoughts that had come into words and actions as wrong karmas and created issues in life. An antidote for wrong thoughts is a set of right and pure thoughts and karmas which can now resolve those issues. Your present could have spiralled towards wrong karmas of creating hurt, resentment or trauma. But consciously creating right thoughts will take you towards the right karmas of forgiveness, understanding and compassion.

The Art of Dying

Hypothetically, suppose we come to know that we will leave the body in five hours from now. What would we want to do before leaving? Talk to the people we care about, tell everyone that we love them, thank them for all that they have done for us, seek forgiveness and offer forgiveness. Getting five hours of advance notice is wishful thinking, considering that most people do not even get five seconds. This makes it imperative that we settle karmic accounts and clean the soul daily. Otherwise, we will be carrying hurt, anger, revenge or rejection with us into the next birth. Our karmic accounts with those souls will get carried forward as well. When we meet them in a new lifetime, that meeting will begin on a note of negative energy exchange. Let us make it a daily practice to thank, appreciate, seek forgiveness and offer forgiveness.

Pay attention to create the right karma always, irrespective of how others behave, challenging situations, what other people say, how others live and work and what others achieve. Practise right ways of being, thinking, behaving, living and working. Live by the highest ethics, values and principles, not by the definitions of 'normal' as decided by others. Let societal expectations not influence any of your decisions. Set your priorities right when it comes to care: self, family and then work.

Remain aware of the truth that you always knew: when we leave the body, people do not go with us, what they did does not go with us, only how we felt and behaved goes with us as our karma. What we achieved and how much we earned is left behind, how we worked and how we earned goes with us. The perfect beautiful body does not go with us, how we treated our body goes with us. Society does not go with us, how we cared and served it goes with us. **So the only two aspects that create the quality of our present life and go with us into subsequent lifetimes as an eternal recording are our sanskars and karmas.**

Just as you strive to settle financial transactions of borrowing or lending, keep your emotional and karmic transactions settled too. Do not wait for people to change. Do not wait for situations to get resolved. Settle the karmic account by blessing them. Living this way keeps karmic accounts clear, the mind sorted and the soul cleansed. And when the moment comes to move forward on a new journey, the soul transitions with ease and dignity because there will be no karmic strings holding it back.

Live every moment of your life as if it is your last moment, for the Art of Dying is indeed the Art of Living.

Acknowledgements

I am extremely grateful to the **Brahma Kumaris World Spiritual Organization** for shaping this work and bringing this book to fruition. Quite literally, every word written in these pages is an offshoot of what has been lovingly shared and taught there. I am merely an instrument in compiling the knowledge together and expressing it in the form of this book.

In a lead-up to this book, two beautiful souls have played a big role: **Brother Suresh Oberoi** and **Sister Kanupriya**, the incredible hosts of the television show *Awakening With Brahma Kumaris*. They became the voice of the people as they put forth insightful questions and personal experiences in honest ways. Those engaging conversations brought out spiritual solutions to practical issues. This book carries the same flavour, that of explaining a logical and comfortable way to ingrain spiritual principles in daily life.

Over the last two decades, millions of souls from different ages, faiths and backgrounds have joined the journey of *Awakening...* show. Several of them turned into 'students of life', taking notes of what was discussed. They applied the knowledge in their personal situations and created miracles like healing from mental health issues, recovering from physical ailments, overcoming addictions, changing emotional patterns of thinking and behaving, and harmonizing relationships. This book has picked up the threads of their questions and experiences.

I thank **BK Arathi** who assisted in transcribing and putting the content together. She was diligent in taking inputs for all the information that had to be shared in the book and the way it had to be presented.

I thank **Mamatha Ramesh** for editing the book. Her timely support, skillfulness and inputs are appreciated.

About the Author

Brahma Kumari (BK) Sister Shivani, a Rajyog Meditation practitioner for over 25 years has become a household name for her refreshing and pragmatic take on life. The Government of India has honored her with 'Nari Shakti Puraskaar', the highest civilian award for women in the country, for transforming human behaviours. Her spiritual TV show 'Awakening with Brahma Kumaris' which began in 2007 has aired over 2,000 episodes. It is empowering millions to raise their emotional quotient, harmonize relationships, create leadership qualities, and experience a meditative lifestyle. Since 2017, she has been appointed as a Goodwill Ambassador by the World Psychiatric Association.

30 Years *of*

 HarperCollins *Publishers* India

At HarperCollins, we believe in telling the best stories and finding the widest possible readership for our books in every format possible. We started publishing 30 years ago; a great deal has changed since then, but what has remained constant is the passion with which our authors write their books, the love with which readers receive them, and the sheer joy and excitement that we as publishers feel in being a part of the publishing process.

Over the years, we've had the pleasure of publishing some of the finest writing from the subcontinent and around the world, and some of the biggest bestsellers in India's publishing history. Our books and authors have won a phenomenal range of awards, and we ourselves have been named Publisher of the Year the greatest number of times. But nothing has meant more to us than the fact that millions of people have read the books we published, and somewhere, a book of ours might have made a difference.

As we step into our fourth decade, we go back to that one word – a word which has been a driving force for us all these years.

Read.

Harper
Collins

HARPER
PERENNIAL

HARPER
BUSINESS

HARPER
BLACK

हार्पर
हिन्दी

HarperCollins
Children'sBooks

HARPER
DESIGN

HARPER
VANTAGE

Harper
Sport